CREATING CONNECTIONS

CREATING CONNECTIONS

Inspire your child to thrive in their learning

Rachel Stewart

Published in 2023 by Amba Press, Melbourne, Australia
www.ambapress.com.au

© Rachel Stewart 2023

All rights reserved. No part of this book may be reproduced or transmitted in any form or by any means, electronic or mechanical, including photocopying, recording or by any information storage and retrieval system, without prior permission in writing from the publisher.

Cover design: Tess McCabe
Internal design: Amba Press
Editor: Kathryn Tafra
Printing: IngramSpark

ISBN: 9781922607720 (pbk)
ISBN: 9781922607737 (ebk)

A catalogue record for this book is available from the National Library of Australia.

CONTENTS

Introduction		1
Chapter 1	Reflections	9
Chapter 2	Identity	29
Chapter 3	Transitions	50
Chapter 4	Relationships	68
Chapter 5	Roles and responsibilities	90
Chapter 6	Wellbeing	113
Chapter 7	What is parent engagement in learning?	138
Chapter 8	How can you support learning?	153
Chapter 9	Feedback for learning improvement	183
Chapter 10	Supporting an entrepreneurial mindset	200
Conclusion		217
About the author		219
References		220

INTRODUCTION

If you were born without wings,
do nothing to prevent them from growing.

COCO CHANEL

Raising children is a responsibility none of us can take lightly. When you bring a person into the world, you take on the responsibility of nurturing, caring for, guiding and supporting them. When you think about it, there isn't a lot of time to make a difference in the life of your child between their birth and when they decide to leave the nest. And, whether we want to admit it or not, we only get one chance at making the most of this opportunity.

Much like planting a seed that eventually grows into a tree, raising a child requires intentional care and attention. A tree, like a child, needs nurturing, the chance to spread its branches and ground its roots. It may need to weather many storms, survive through the seasons and endure sunny days, dull and wet days, and everything in between. Tree and a child need preparation to have the strength and the foundation to sprout new buds, to flourish, and to grow into a mature adult with the ability to survive and thrive.

It's possible that this task you've taken on as parent or carer has presented some challenges as well as curiosities. Perhaps you are not sure of your role in your child's life once they begin their journey through school and into a whole other world of influences. Perhaps you need some guidance around how to manage the changes up ahead, what to expect and how you can effectively guide and support your child through them. If this is why you find yourself reading this book, you've come to the right place.

I have written this book for you; a book I wish I'd had when my own children were going through their formal education. Instead, I had to learn as I went, navigating the transitions and many changes that occurred along the way. My observations and experiences during that time have formed some of the wisdom I wish to share with you so you can feel supported and confident in knowing what your role is, how things will change for you and how you can manage these changes.

My story is unique, as is yours. Each of us is navigating life at our own pace and in our own way. There may be some information in this book that resonates with you and there may be experiences you've had that are quite different to mine. There is no perfect answer in how to navigate life but I have learned that life is like discovering a treasure each day. There is so much to learn about ourselves, about others, about our world, and finding the jewels in each day is a gift we are given. Life doesn't happen to you, it happens for you and it is up to you to discover and enjoy the moments, the experiences and the lessons that teach you the answers to the mysteries of life. Most often those answers lie within.

During the times you share with your children. you can begin to understand yourself at a deeper level. They are an extension and a reflection of you and they have been brought to you for a reason.

This is why it is important for you to be aware and understand yourself and your role as your child moves through their learning journey. When it comes to raising children and supporting their learning, you matter more than you may realise. You are also like a tree – your branches keep sprouting and growing; you keep learning and developing your own strengths and skills as a leader within your family. You may feel like all your learning is complete, but there is still growth occurring every day.

As the seasons change and your life phases come and go, you may drop leaves, lie dormant and regenerate. As you move through life, it's important you continue to grow, learn, expand and nurture yourself so that you can feel grounded, steady and in alignment with yourself. This will ensure you are able to manage the ups and downs of life, and are capable of continuing to plant seeds of hope in the lives of your children and others.

This book is not intended to tell you how to parent. Rather, it is an invitation to consider that parenting to support future generations is our responsibility, because children are the future of the planet – parenting should be intentional, acknowledged and valued, not only by others but most importantly by you. Nurturing yourself and being aware of who you are will help you to carry out as best you can the role of parent.

Much of what I will share with you as you move through each chapter relates to my own experiences as a mother of three children, my personal journey from childhood to adulthood, as well as my professional journey and what I've observed needs to change in our world to ensure every child flourishes. I look at my life from various perspectives and will share what I have observed and learned so that I can support you to be aware, connected and engaged in your child's education, so that they in turn are well equipped to manage the next phases of their life. This is one of the main roles you have as a parent, and it has been somewhat overlooked or not a valued priority in education. It is time that it was – to support children in the best way possible. This is my passion and my purpose.

While working with educators and parents in my children's primary school several years ago, I realised the vast need for improvement of relationships in the home, within schools and between home and school.

I have spent more than a decade working with schools, developing their internal culture and introducing new ways to improve understanding of adults' roles in the lives of children. This has included coaching and workshopping how to develop partnerships with each other, and educating staff and parents about the importance of their unique relationship and how it impacts children's learning.

Effective partnerships are demonstrated when we are providing positive, considered, conscious and intentional role modelling for children. This will assist you, as their main influencers, to have the ability to provide your children with a stable foundation, setting them up for a future with the potential for many personal and professional achievements.

For teachers and parents, working together as partners doesn't necessarily mean that everything is going to be smooth sailing. There are challenges within every human relationship, especially the relationship with yourself. Where there are good times, there are also challenges that test our strength and our ability to resolve them. Within any relationship, we must learn to be vulnerable, especially in our relationship with our children, to provide the nurturing they need. How we manage our actions and consequent reactions provides the modelling our children emulate in their own behaviours, to be able to acknowledge and manage emotions and their own relationships as they progress through school and into adulthood.

I am driven to help children by enabling the connection between parent and child to thrive, both before they arrive at school and once they begin their journey through the education system and beyond. Another important connection between adults and children encompasses the teacher–child relationship, which is most influential throughout a child's education and can have a major impact on their passion and motivation to learn. You will explore how to support this connection in more detail as you move through the book.

Relationship modelling begins when we are children, as we observe our parents, other family members and people we connect with in the local and broader community. It is our relationship with ourselves that needs more focus if we are to understand others. More often than not, we leave ourselves out of the equation and may rely on others to make us happy or to fill any gaps or voids. In my own experience, I recognised this was happening in my relationships and that I needed to go inward to understand myself and improve my connection with my children. The difference this made to the family dynamics and how I coped through the numerous changes and transitions my children went through was incredible. Therefore, I have focused the book on helping you understand what creating connections means for you, for your relationship with your children, and how this impacts your family and their learning.

Possibly one of the most common things on the minds of parents as they fumble their way through the school journey is whether their children are going to make it in the big wide world once their formal education is complete. I had these thoughts often myself as my own children began this journey. I was so busy with raising them, working and being everything to everyone, all of a sudden I realised I had lost sight of the moments that were taking place around me. I was focusing too much on the future instead of managing and enjoying the now. I knew I had to make some changes and take a bird's eye view of my behaviour and my relationship with myself and how this was impacting my children.

In 2012 I experienced a massive shift in my life as I began reflecting on the way I was presenting myself as a person and as a parent, and on how I was raising my children. I was questioning my role in their lives once they started school. What would my role be once I had got them to the point where they could be sent from home to another environment to learn? How would my role in teaching them change, and what would I need to teach them? I answered these questions by reflecting on my own personal journey. I thought carefully about how I wanted to guide my children towards the skills and strengths they would need to survive in this ever changing world. I will share the process of reflection I went through, to support you in creating an environment at home that inspires learning and an intentional way of thinking about how you approach your children as they learn and grow.

There are many shifts occurring in the world that challenge our beliefs and values. The views of others can challenge family values and what you would like to teach or pass down to your children. These include changes in the way we embrace the diversity of others while also allowing people the freedom to be themselves and have a voice, changes in technology, employment and the way we work, in communication, changes in climate, the way we approach our relationship with the environment and a strong focus on identity and having a sense of belonging on Earth.

Children have access to more forms of media from a young age and seem to be more aware of what's happening in the world via the content they are consuming. So much information needing to be processed constantly by the brain results in changes to the way we learn and decipher information, and at times it tests our ability to stay focused. All of these changes can impact children and how they view the world, how they learn at school, how they form relationships and how to manage all the information that is competing for their attention. There are shifts in education, particularly since the Covid-19 pandemic, with online and hybrid models of learning being undertaken by many universities and schools to cater for changes in where, how, why and what we learn.

People around the world are realising they have more choices in how and where they want to live, work and behave. For example, shifts in technology are impacting manufacturing and many different industries – such as the car, building, mining, farming and food industries – that once relied on human physical strength. Robotics and automated machinery are replacing humans to carry out tasks. Educators need to shift focus to ensure what is being taught at school is preparing children for their future professional and personal lives. You as parent also need to be aware of the changing nature of work and living that your children will encounter in the future.

The World Economic Forum (2022) researched some of the world's largest companies, who shared that the skills children will need in the future – and therefore must be learning now – include:

- **Creativity** and the ability to solve meaningful problems in new ways, to think imaginatively across disciplines.
- **Digital skills** and the ability to master new forms of digital technology especially algorithm design and data handling.
- **Collaboration** and the ability to work with others to perform complex tasks and adjust actions in relation to other people's needs.
- **Global citizenship** – a universal respect for people from other cultures and the willingness to embrace diversity and inclusion.
- **Environmental stewardship** – understanding the fragility and finiteness of natural ecosystems and how we can interact with them in sustainable ways.

As parents guiding your children through their education, these skills can provide areas of focus for you as you think intentionally about your child's current life. This may include the influences they are surrounded by, how and what they are learning and how this may impact their future.

As you know, one of the biggest shifts in the world occurred in 2020, when a sudden pandemic impacted everyone on the planet. Education was affected by the Covid-19 pandemic in new ways. Suddenly parents were asked to be partners alongside teachers, which ironically is what five decades of research had been suggesting educators should have been doing well before the pandemic. Teachers had to rapidly switch to online learning and had to work out how to engage students who were feeling the strain of being at home for so long, away from friends and family and the security they knew through those networks. Some children preferred the home environment and the safety of family, leading to many children struggling to adjust back to the school environment once restrictions eased.

For me, the pandemic came like a bolt of lightning and caused massive upheaval in my life. It shifted my way of thinking and my way of life – the fear and uncertainty it brought caused me to take stock of my priorities. It forced me to look at the pace of life and shift perspectives, to slow down and appreciate every day, every moment, and the precious time I have, especially with my children. I took many lessons from this time, as I'm sure you have. I will share with you through this book some of those lessons. Time with your children can open your eyes to the wonderful learning happening every day for them and how you as parents have an important role to play in their education by supporting them at home. What they learn from you and other people you surround them with has a huge impact on how they are able to learn at school, not only academically but socially and emotionally, physically and spiritually.

I must clarify that I am not a child psychologist, scholar, or doctor of philosophy, nor am I a school teacher. I am first and foremost a parent, seeker of learning opportunities, lover of nature and creativity, and a passionate explorer of how we can make changes in our lives to improve the future for our children. I am also a transformational coach and learning facilitator with extensive training and experience in shifting mindsets and perspectives in how we can manage our thought processes and be more in control of our minds to overcome challenges and cope with change.

I prefer not to give myself a label but I am simply a messenger, spreading the news that we can shift the culture in our schools and homes to support children to thrive in a world that is desperately hurt and trying to heal. I will explore with you how you can support your children to be the solution, the designers, the next generation of truth seekers and changers to heal and secure the future of the planet.

My professional background was initially in graphic design, marketing and advertising, where I used critical and creative thinking to analyse and solve problems, then visually represent the solution and communicate messages to an audience. Through my work, I always seek to find answers. I have discovered that we need to look at ourselves more closely. We need to consider what makes us tick, what inspires us, what challenges us, how we can heal ourselves, what our children really need from us and what they need to be taught, and also what our roles are in their lives.

Throughout this book I have provided insights and suggestions on how to navigate various areas you can focus on as your child's main influence in their learning and development; how you can guide them towards their passions and interests in a way that aligns with them as a unique individual; how you can open their eyes to the wonders of the world and the moments you can share with them along their journey. My aim is to help you make the days count in the short time you will have with your children while they are young. It is a shared journey between you, your child and their educators, as well as the extended family and friends you may have. You are called upon to support and guide them to discover for themselves where their path will lead.

As you make your way through this book, you may choose to read according to your circumstances – with a focus on one child, or on all of your children if you have more than one. Remember that everyone is on their own unique journey of discovery of self, of their children, of each of the changes that constantly occur each day. This guide will support you on that journey. You may have to discover answers yourself along the way. I will prompt you with questions to broaden your understanding of yourself and help you to think about being more intentional when it comes to supporting your child's learning. Some questions may challenge your thinking and invite conversation or self reflection. This book is intended to awaken you to acknowledge the value of you and your role as the most important guide and support for your children as they move through school and life.

Chapter 1

REFLECTIONS

Where my learning journey began

Don't count the days, make the days count.

MOHAMMED ALI

I never realised the amazing power of being human until I had children.

The experience of bringing another being into the world is unforgettable and so profound. Every person who has experienced becoming a parent for the first time will have a different story and experience. Whatever your story might be, there are always choices in how you create new experiences that make a difference in the lives of you and your children.

As soon as my first child was born, she looked right through me, into my soul, with her big, beautiful dark eyes. It was an emotional and spiritual experience that I had never felt before, yet it felt very familiar. A very deep connection came over me at that moment. I wish I'd understood at the time what that feeling meant and how the connection with another soul, my child, would completely change my life and be all consuming in my new role as parent.

Children bring absolute, pure love. Life is never the same as they offer love to us in such an unselfish, unconditional way. They, in turn, look for and bring out love in us. It is a powerful beginning to a life when a child loves and is loved in return.

Following the euphoria of giving birth, I suddenly had an overwhelming feeling that everything I do, everything I say and every move I make influences the very innocent being I just gave the gift of life to. It was quite daunting, especially the very first time, and the second and then the third!

Newborns seem helpless and they have a purity that is challenging to sustain. Newborns are pure essence with no ego or external influences present. For a short while, they don't get angry, jealous, frustrated, worried or anxious. When they cry, they are communicating their basic human needs. More often than not, they are seeking love and connection and this continues as they grow.

Over the past two decades, as a parent of three children, I have come to recognise that each experience, every milestone, every life-changing moment is a lesson for myself just as much as it is a lesson for my children. Influenced by my own experiences as a child growing up through to adulthood, I have unconsciously passed on various traits and beliefs that my own parents and grandparents passed on to me. The main influences of family, society and culture are most often passed on to children and can impact their learning and development more than their formal education.

When it comes to your children's development, it is fascinating to observe the constant growth and learning that happens every day before your eyes. From those wonderful moments as babies, to their first steps and the first words, to the precious and profound things they say to you, each is a growth moment.

However, it is easy to forget as they get older that there continue to be many moments that provide your child with opportunities for growth. Sometimes when children begin school, our focus can shift to the final results on the school report, the next stage, the next age, the next level, the next test or exam, the next day, the next month, year, and so on. Rather than counting down the days until Friday, until the next holiday, until the next birthday, we can instead be conscious of making each precious moment count.

So why is this important to be aware of? I recognised as the years flew by with my own children that I hadn't taken enough time to really be in the moment with them. Not only that, I had also neglected myself in many ways – by focusing so much on their needs, activities and other demands,

I neglected my own self care. Over the past few years I have focused more on my awareness of myself, becoming more present in each moment, conscious of my thoughts and actions so I could be the person I wanted to be for myself and others.

As a parent you have so many hats to wear that it can be easy to lose sight of who you actually are, how you're showing up every day and what you are teaching your children. It is important to be aware of yourself and your values as you journey along with your children to guide them with their learning. Throughout this book I will share with you how you can find time to do this, and why it is important. But first I will share my learning journey over the past five decades.

My appetite for learning grew enormously while writing this book, as I reflected on my life and the many lessons I learned on my journey through childhood, my teenage years, and as I became an adult and a parent.

Through my children's eyes - spending time observing their wonderment, their innocence and observations of life - I feel I have learned so much more than any formal education taught me. They are life. They bring us back to life. This is life and we are here to uncover and enjoy the process rather than trying to control the outcome. Not always an easy task.

I became aware of my own role in my children's learning very early on. I realised the responsibility that comes with teaching them how to make good choices and instilling in them a love of wonder, creativity and curiosity from a very young age. What took me a while to realise, though, was how my own sense of self - self worth, self love and self awareness - impacted my children energetically, physiologically and psychologically.

Once I realised this, I recognised the need to understand myself on a different level. This was when I discovered that to be the person I wanted to be, I needed to practice self care and so began to explore self mastery. This included looking deeply into all areas of my life and where I might improve. In my relationships with my children, I discovered I needed to learn how to manage my emotions, reactions and responses - to them and to life's constant changes and challenging situations. This was the first step towards awareness of who I truly am, how I behave and respond to different situations, and who I want to be. It was through this process that I came to understand and take responsibility for the impact my behaviour has on my children, and to explore and understand my unique relationship with each of them. I knew there were things I needed to explore further about myself so I could effectively nurture them and their growth.

I wasn't afraid to change myself, as my life has been full of changes – no doubt yours has been also, but change can be daunting for many people. Perhaps it was my rural upbringing and various pivotal, sometimes traumatic moments in my life that helped me to navigate changes. I learned to understand and appreciate the simplicity of life, particularly in nature, where everything is constantly changing yet always returning to the way it was. I guess you could say I was a keen observer of nature and how it is a metaphor for how to live life. Knowing that sunny days can change suddenly to cold and dark cloudy days, but also knowing that the sun always shines again. This is the rollercoaster ride that is life as we know it, and knowing how to go with the flow of the unknown alongside the predictable is a skill we all learn as we go. Our role as parents is to guide our children to navigate this ebb and flow, while also learning how to do it effectively ourselves.

While writing this book, exploring the impact of home life on school learning, I reflected on my own experiences as a child and how they impacted my learning both personally and at school. Life for me began in a nuclear family of mum, dad and four children. From the age of three I lived on 25 acres in a rural part of my home state of Victoria. Life was relatively carefree and easy, with plenty of time spent outdoors, playing sports and navigating different sibling relationships with my brothers and younger sister.

Our seemingly idyllic world was not without its sad times. We lived near a large state forest so almost every summer there was a bushfire. I think we evacuated into the nearest town at least half a dozen times for safety. While these were quite traumatic experiences, during these times I witnessed the generosity of neighbours and friends as they reached out to others in the community. There always seemed to be someone who cared and who was willing to help during difficult times. This was my introduction to volunteering and the importance of the strength of community.

When I reached the age of nine, my parents separated. I was forced, as were my siblings and my mother, to navigate the challenges of my parents' divorce with little or no support to understand what was happening. That same year my best friend left the school, but no-one told me what happened to her. One day she was there, the next she was gone with no explanation. Then, towards the end of the same year, my maternal grandmother died. This was an extremely difficult time for all of us but there was no support or conversations about what had happened and how to process the grief. We children were left to our own devices to learn how to overcome the sadness that comes with loss and change.

After these three major life-changing events, we were forced to move into the local town, which was another huge change. We had been so used to playing outside, having space and freedom, and even though we would squabble and had our differences, we had been together, learning from each other, having fun and sharing special times.

As a shy redhead with freckles, I experienced bullying and had trouble making friends at primary school. On top of that, having a single mother wasn't very common. I felt quite the outsider and wasn't sure who I could turn to. My saving grace was that I was creative. I could draw and design from a very young age, escaping the adult issues that were going on around me and creating new worlds that felt safe and more real. It was my way of coping and expressing myself. This was my own way of dealing with trauma, even though at the time I didn't realise that's what was happening and that my brain was being wired to respond to these major life changes. Little did I know at the time how it would impact me as an adult.

Every day I would indulge in my passion for drawing. There was hardly a day that I didn't have a pencil and paper in my hand. I truly believe my ability for writing and creative thinking came from often having time to myself, and the space and ability to find peace, to zone out, be in my own world to create and discover my talents. I still enjoy my own company and the opportunity to have peace and stillness in my life to create, meditate and connect with myself and my intuition. That special place that belongs only to me.

In my teenage years my mother remarried and I became part of a larger, blended family of ten children. This was another momentous change. We were put in a position out of our control, having to build relationships with a new dad and six new siblings who had also been through quite a lot of trauma in their young lives. It wasn't easy for any of us, but my stepfather eventually became a friend and confidante. Moving into this new family dynamic was difficult, but over time it proved to be a blessing as we learned so much about each other and how to get along and be a part of something that was quite unique at the time. While this blended family structure is more common now, it was fairly unusual when I was young.

The lessons I learned from being part of such a large, blended family are many. We spent a lot of time together, so we had to navigate different personalities while riding motorbikes, playing football and cricket, camping, fishing, swimming in the local creek, climbing trees, helping with the sheep, raising chickens and spending time at the gently flowing stream and our huge dam. We could run around and make up games without fear, and our parents didn't seem to worry about us. If we fell over, we helped each other or we just got back up again. There was an innocence about being on the land and learning from nature. Mum wasn't always around, so we learned to solve our own issues and be resilient.

In many ways I was very lucky because I was able to experience the city when we would stay with my dad every fortnight. He would often take us to different places and show us the sites of Melbourne. We learned how to navigate the streets and had the opportunity to go to other great places that would usually be saved for school excursions. I guess you could say I had the best of both worlds, learning about the city and the country. My teenage self saw this as an unpleasant experience but once I became an adult I could appreciate the positives. I made the conscious choice not to let my past perceptions of challenging times impact my life in a negative way. Everything happens to teach you something – often about others, but mostly about yourself.

As I moved through school I had some fantastic art and design teachers but was discouraged by most of the adults around me from pursuing a career in creative arts. This was confusing for me so I decided not to listen to the naysayers as I was determined to forge my own path. And so I did and still do.

I studied graphic design and advertising and went on to run two businesses – first in design and then as a coach and consultant in parent engagement. I continue to create my own work and life path as an entrepreneur. I only realised through my recent journey of self discovery that all the challenges I had faced and overcome as a young person had given me the ability, grit, perseverance and drive to create my own way of living and working. This is where I found freedom, to be myself and discover my own story.

Observation is a skill I gained very early in my childhood and it has served me well over time, particularly in different aspects of my career. I was a fairly quiet child and was often watching, listening and learning from others. This gave me a deep sense of empathy and what is now called emotional intelligence. I believe my resilience to cope with trauma and change has developed through the many great times I've experienced, as well as my ability to overcome the many challenging times.

As I raised my own children through their early years, I really enjoyed being their main influence and setting the groundwork, or foundations, for them to move into their next learning environment. I had an understanding that to effectively guide my children to become capable adults, there were times when I needed to be available to them and times when I must step back and let them discover themselves. I knew the early years were the most important foundation so I based my work at home so I could be there when my children started eating solids, took their first steps and spoke their first words. I was able to share special moments with them, guiding them towards their next milestones.

We loved reading, going on excursions, spending time in the park and observing nature, talking and singing, sharing meals and playing games. We went camping and spent time with friends and family on the farm and exposing them to various experiences. This was a busy time but one that I really miss because we were so connected. During that time I was able to learn about each of my children, who they were and how to navigate each of their personalities, even though at times this was challenging. Once they reached school age, I knew they were ready to transition to their next learning experiences, but I hoped to continue learning with them along the way.

When I first experienced the school journey with my eldest child, I soon observed that many things about the school environment hadn't changed or evolved since I was a student. This surprised me as I felt the culture of school might have evolved over time. The more I explored and worked in education as a consultant or "critical friend" for schools, the more I observed cultural aspects that needed to change. Yet there was a resistance to change, especially when it came to the relationships and communication between home and school, and enabling parents to stay on that journey with their children.

I initially observed the experience of school almost as a bystander, like looking from the outside of a snowdome into the tiny village where the snow was falling. I could see the children running through the village but I wasn't there with them. The children seemed to be learning in a separate environment, with little or no connection to home life. It became clear to me that parents were often kept at a distance and left in the dark when it came to their child's whole other world at school. I realised I had a strong desire to break down the barriers between the two most important learning environments for children, to enable them to thrive across all areas of life.

Since I first observed this, I have been exploring both of these learning environments and the different roles adults have in providing safe and collaborative learning opportunities in each of them. The shift to online learning during the pandemic exposed the impact of the different learning environments on children, many of whom struggle with the structures and pressures of formal school learning. With increases in behavioural challenges in school classrooms and playgrounds, school refusals, and children suffering crippling anxiety, particularly since the pandemic, it is clear there needs to be changes in the way we are supporting children.

This is particularly the case in Victoria, my home state, which saw an increase in children's anxiety as

> lockdowns and remote learning drove a surge in calls to the Kids Helpline in 2020 and higher numbers in 2021. A Mission Australia youth survey found more than one-quarter of young people met the criteria for experiencing psychological distress in 2020. School refusal, or school phobia, isn't just children skipping classes. It's linked to underlying issues such as depression, separation anxiety, and anxiety. Monash Health child psychiatrist Dr Michael Gordon said the pandemic had led to socialisation problems and emotional delays, and an increase in children with eating disorders, suicidal behaviours, psychosis and school refusal (O'Connell and Watterston 2022).

School refusal is on the increase and recent research has indicated there are thousands of children dropping out of the school system altogether. "At least 50,000 young Australians have 'disappeared' from the education system nationwide", according to a report from the University of Melbourne. The report, *Those Who Disappear: The Australian education problem nobody wants to talk about* (2022), was written by Megan O'Connell and Dr Jim Watterston to shed light on the issue of young people of compulsory school age across Australia who are not participating in an education program of any type. The report also proposes solutions for how to prevent this trend from continuing. Dr Watterston said, "the issue is a serious educational crisis that has until now been largely ignored.

Young Australians of all ages have been able to detach themselves from the education system and we don't know who they are, where they are, or why they remain hidden."

While for a long time parents have chosen alternative methods of education, such as home schooling, distance learning or other alternatives to mainstream schools, the causes of the issue of school truancy are not fully clear, nor have they necessarily been investigated properly.

Many children have always struggled through school, including myself. I wasn't suited to all the different subject areas and needed further support. Back then, there was no extra support for children and if parents didn't help or were disengaged, many children fell through the cracks. Unfortunately this still happens today as the role that parents have to support learning is not often explained to parents or enabled by the school. The important connection and consistent approach to learning between each of the environments of home and school are not always prioritised once a child is participating in formal and structured education. This contributes to the parents' sense of disconnect, as they begin to gradually feel disempowered. Instead of fulfilling their important role to guide and support learning at home, they rely on educators to teach children many skills that can, and often should, be learned at home.

Through my own observations and research over the past twelve years, I have come to recognise that this may be the result of schools continuing to adopt an antiquated model of parent involvement at school. This places the parent in the position of volunteer at school and limits their role at home to overseeing homework, rather than supporting their children by engaging effectively to support learning at home. Through my observations and in researching the past five decades of evidence-based parent engagement approaches, I recognised a lack of training or awareness of the roles of parent and teacher when it comes to working together to support students.

In addition to this, as one of the missing pieces in education, school and home are only two of many learning environments that children are now navigating. Children are exposed to online content and communities that compete for their attention and focus. Parents are often learning how to navigate these demands – many of which were not as prevalent when we were children. Often, as a parent, you may feel like it's a minefield to understand what your role is, to decipher all the information available, and even to know whether you are capable of navigating this journey with your children. But you are absolutely capable. We will explore in this book how you can manage and understand your role in guiding and supporting your children through the many exciting adventures and experiences they will have along the way. You can make a conscious choice to stay with them and walk alongside educators to achieve this.

A school can form an important part of your children's life and network as they begin to make friends and have a sense of connection, to spread their wings and understand how it feels to belong to a community. Wellbeing plays a major part in the lives of children, in how they are able to focus and function socially at school and in other learning environments. A sense of connection and belonging is related to wellbeing, especially when it comes to developing relationships and friendships at school. This is why it's critical for parents to be included on the school journey – many of the lessons you will be navigating with your child will relate to their wellbeing, particularly their friendships and socialisation skills, as well as their academic learning.

Moving to a new learning environment is an important part of a child's growth, but it can result in a disconnect between parent and child that is often overlooked. Over the past few years, parents who have wanted to stay connected with their children have been labelled by the media and some parenting experts as being overbearing, as helicopter or tiger parents, or as needing to stay attached to their children and to control their every move. "Most labels are designed to induce guilt, but they all have a place at some point in our children's lives. I adopt helicopter parenting during playtime if I think one child is being treated unfairly and when it comes to extra-curricular activities I admit I have to quell my inner tiger." (Ricca Smith 2023) The need for control or being overbearing may not be the intention of parents. They may simply want to be a part of their child's learning journey, to be able to support and guide them rather than be separated from their school life. It's important to reflect on how you can remain connected while also giving your child the freedom to grow and become independent. Consistency, communication and a genuine partnership between home and school can contribute to enabling you to support your children as they navigate each learning environment.

You have a critical role to play in your children's lives at home to encourage and enhance the learning skills needed to support their ability to learn effectively at school. When they come home from school, you will see glimpses of what has happened – sometimes they may actually share with you what they are learning or experiencing in their interactions with teachers and other children. Perhaps the most important tool for you in your role to support them is being conscious of your responses and reactions to what they share with you. There will be things they navigate in the playground and classroom that you will not witness, but you may have to manage the aftermath of this at home. It is during these times you will need to be self aware in your responses.

One of your most important roles is to regularly tune in with your child; to observe and communicate with them. Try to be present so they know they can come to you, share with you and feel supported.

I enjoy watching my three children and how they are learning every day, not only at school but also at home. I delight in listening to the conversations between them and I enjoy the different relationships they have with each other. Creating safe spaces and opportunities for interactions at home supports your child to develop essential social skills they then take with them to school. These are called "joint attention" skills and involve enabling children to learn how to develop eye contact, to be able to identify different objects and people, to read other people's emotions and to respond to others in conversation, verbally or through actions. Even though at times sibling interactions are challenging and children attempt to test boundaries, this is still an essential and normal part of their growth and development. It is through these experiences that they are learning their greatest lessons – how to manage themselves and relate with others. I, too, learned how to observe and respond to their behaviour, pointing them in the right direction in how to treat others and how to show respect. My responses to the information they share with me is top of mind during our conversations. Through tuning in and reflecting on my observations of what they are saying, I can tell what mood they are in, when to tread carefully, and when and how to respond or remain impartial when there is a disagreement. I try not to overreact or lecture, but to simply listen, observe and respond appropriately.

Your children are your greatest teachers and they in turn seek you as theirs. I see this as the key to providing opportunities to stay connected with your children on their learning journey. Each child is a unique individual and sometimes the qualities or habits we observe in them, that we may not like, can provide us with an opportunity to reflect on ourselves. Sometimes how others behave can be a reflection of our own behaviours and attitudes, like looking in a mirror. It is only through an awareness of ourselves that we have the ability to see this. For example, if you are feeling grumpy or agitated, you can often see this reflected back at you in your children. They respond to your energy and what you project onto them. They can also do this to you, so acute observation is required to understand the reasons behind their behaviour or attitude towards you. As a parent you will often be on the receiving end of their projections because you are their safe place – you may have unconditional love for them but you still need to set and explain boundaries for how you want them to treat you and others.

I find these observations fascinating and yet, for most of us, we don't realise that all of these moments are learning experiences. They guide us like signposts, giving us instructions on what we need to change or do next.

As you move through this book, remind yourself that this is a unique journey of discovery of both yourself and each of your children. There are so many lessons to learn along the way and being open to this will help you to get through each stage of the journey.

The role of parent, as you know, is physically, mentally, spiritually and intellectually demanding. It constantly delights but also tests your resolve, resilience and emotional stability. Having the tools to manage these areas of your life means you're able to enjoy parenting and your extremely important role as supporter of your child's learning, growth, wellbeing and development. One of the first steps in managing each of the different areas of your life is to understand your own journey from childhood. Now that you have heard my story and how it has led me to where I am today, it's time to reflect on your story, how it has shaped you and how you would like to create stronger connections with your children by working on yourself.

"I want my children to be happy"

> Ironically enough when you make peace with the fact that the purpose in life is not happiness, but rather experience and growth, happiness comes as a natural byproduct. When you aren't seeking it as an objective, it will find its way to you.
>
> UNKNOWN

Through my familial relationships, friendships and professional life, in researching, coaching and consulting, I've learned that what most parents desire for their children is happiness. Happiness is a concept that sometimes seems attainable, however – despite most people seeking it endlessly and most often from external sources – it is ultimately a perception and is unique for every person. Happiness means different things to each individual, whether it be material things that make you happy, another person, indulgences, simple pleasures, being treated well, or seeing your child grow and learn. Happiness is ultimately a feeling that we seek for ourselves and our children, and feelings are essentially an internal experience, often influenced by external factors. Unless you are able to find happiness within yourself, external factors are not able to fill that void.

While happiness is certainly worth striving for, the reality is your child won't be happy all the time and neither will you because the reality is that most people don't really know themselves or do the internal work needed to be truly happy. Life presents many obstacles to what we perceive as happiness, in the form of opposites occurring in each moment. Without sadness we can't experience happiness – because you need to experience both to understand the difference between them. Learning to navigate the dualities of life, the ups and the downs of parenting and of life in general, is your greatest learning experience and one to pass on to your children. Ultimately, the happiness you seek comes from within and discovering this is a lifelong learning process.

One of the greatest lessons I've learned as I've grown into the many roles of adulthood is to prioritise my own self love and self care, including my mindset and expectations of myself and others. It took me a long while to realise this, but when you are responsible for other humans each day (as a parent, teacher or other caregiver), your presence in the moment, your health and strength of character, your resilience and healthy mind and body are all critical ingredients for getting through each day. How you manage these on a daily basis also impacts your children and how they look to you for guidance in how to cope in daily life.

What does self care look like?

Creating change begins with an intentional mindset and developing habits that are designed to keep you on the path to achieve what you are seeking. When we create good habits and stick with them it gives us a sense of control over our life, a sense of achievement and satisfaction. Prioritising your own health and wellbeing will have a positive impact on yourself and those you love and care for. Here are some of the ways I practice self care, and suggestions for you to begin:

- **Routines** – Create a simple routine every morning such as meditating for about 10-15 minutes. This will help you be more centred, relaxed and be ready for the day.
- **Energy release** – Breathing exercises can help remove energy that has built up during the night and to feel more energised for the day ahead. There are many apps available that provide guided meditations and breathing exercises. A shower in the morning can also release energy in the body so you are fresh and ready for the day and what it will bring.
- **Exercise** – Take a morning walk or do other outdoor exercise to get into nature and fresh air. This may include listening to music or a podcast as you walk, or simply being in silence, listening to the noises around you and allowing yourself to tune in to your intuition or your 'inner voice'.
- **Writing** – Write an intention or thought for the day in your journal. Ask yourself how you are feeling right now. How do you want to approach the day and what would you like to focus on? Write it down and read it three times to help you remember to carry out this intention through the day. At the end of the day you can reflect on how you stayed true to that intention.
- **Reading** – One thing that often helps me when I am feeling slightly flat or low is to read a paragraph out of a book. More often than not, when I flick open a page and start reading, there is a message in there that gives me something to think about or is a positive affirmation that kick-starts my day. It helps me remember that there is magic to be discovered in each day and that there are messages or signposts showing me the way.
- **Affirmations** – Positive affirmations can help you to feel optimistic as you begin your day and to see and appreciate the great things about yourself, your children and family, and to feel grateful for what you have in life. Life is a gift and even though it can be tough sometimes, the smallest things you are grateful for can be the catalyst for experiencing a feeling of happiness.
- **Reflections** – At the end of each day reflect on one thing that brought you joy (and perhaps ask your children to do this also), you'll soon discover these small moments can bring you happiness.

- **Do something fun** – Sometimes you might catch yourself telling yourself negative stories or feeling down on yourself. This can bring on tension or anxiety that can then lead to other things like feeling unwell, sore or just a feeling of being low or lacking in energy. If you are fully aware of how you are feeling, you have the opportunity to change this by doing something that brings you joy. Listening to music, dancing, listening to or watching a funny show, exercising, or something else that you enjoy can quickly bring you back to the moment. You might then realise that life at that moment isn't so bad and that you have a choice in how you want to feel.

You may have other things that you enjoy doing that are part of your self-care routine. Even if you only take a short amount of time each day due to your busy schedule, it's important to remember to take care of yourself. Other self care methods might include taking a bath or longer shower, listening to your favourite music, calling a friend to chat, going for a coffee, seeing a movie, going dancing, joining a club, going to a comedy show or for dinner, the list is endless. It is important to be able to take time out for you to feel more energised and capable of managing the dualities of life and finding balance and connection within yourself. There is no reason to feel any guilt about looking after yourself. You are the only one who can do this so this needs to be a priority.

Over the past fourteen years I have been learning about the brain and neuroscience to understand my own mind and how to help others through coaching. I have learned (and am still learning) how to manage thoughts, perceptions, patterns, habits and behaviours. One of the most interesting concepts I have learned about, is that of opposites and how to acknowledge them as a way of achieving the happiness we seek. I have learned from inspiring teachers, including Dr John Demartini. Through his coaching program, The Breakthrough Experience, Demartini explained his Law of Contrasts – "whatever you try to escalate, the equal and opposites appear. Society needs a pair of opposite value systems" (2002).

To achieve balance in your life, so you feel more able to manage the opposites, picture a see-saw in your mind. Much like our daily experience, the see-saw moves up and down. One minute your day is going well, the next minute something pops up to challenge you or test you. It might be something one of your children has done or something at work that tests your patience or your strength. Your reaction is a part of the response to this shift in the see-saw. Often we perceive challenges as a problem to solve, an issue or a pain to deal with. There is no avoiding the see-saw, going up and down all the time, but you can find balance in the chaos. The duality of good days and bad days that you constantly have to deal with can be easier when you are able to bring yourself to a place of equilibrium. This means recognising the good in the bad and the bad in the good. To find balance, try viewing every experience as a lesson and seeing what it is trying to teach you. If you view every experience you have – even challenging ones – as necessary to show you something about yourself, you gradually become more aware of how to respond to each experience – good or bad – and what it is showing you that needs attention.

The experiences I share can help you understand why people behave a certain way. This can help you manage the things that are constantly changing and happening in your life and in the lives of those you care for.

There are various reasons why many parents are protective of or fearful for their children and are so focused on the concept of happiness. It is often related to a desire to fulfil core needs and value systems:

According to life and business strategist, Anthony Robbins (2023), humans have six core needs:

Personality needs	1. **Certainty** – the need or desire for clarity, control, balance, authority, success, superiority, power, freedom.
	2. **Uncertainty/variety** – the need or desire for excitement, thrills, drama.
	3. **Significance** – the need or desire to feel valued, a sense of belonging, to feel appreciated, needed, to seek attention, to feel important, validated, superior.
	4. **Love/connection** – the need or desire for belonging, to feel loved and cared for, to feel worthy of love.
Spiritual needs	5 **Growth** – the need or desire for personal and professional growth, ambition, achievement, success; to appear to be successful in every aspect of life.
	6. **Contribution** – the need or desire for giving back to society, being a contributor in the family, in the workplace and society.

According to Dr Joe Dispenza, author of *Breaking the habit of being yourself – how to lose your mind and create a new one* (2013), "these core needs are all connected with our nervous system and can act as a way of motivating us to take action or, on the flip side, can prevent us from allowing life to flow more freely." If we don't receive or achieve what we desire, there are layers of emotions we memorise and store in our limbic brain that arise from past experiences. These memories form our perceptions. These perceptions are related to the responses from the brain when something happens outside of our core needs. In other words, our brain is trying to achieve these needs and when we are not able to achieve them, we can feel out of balance or that something is missing.

Humans can react to their needs not being met with feelings of:

- Unworthiness
- Anger
- Fear
- Anxiety
- Shame
- Self doubt
- Guilt
- Overwhelm
- Tiredness
- Worry
- Frustration.

When our needs are being met we may experience the opposite feelings of:

- Self worth
- Calmness
- Strength
- Centredness
- Pride
- Confidence
- Conviction
- Groundedness
- High energy
- Unconcerned
- Contentedness.

The more focus you place on each of these emotions and the more you believe they are your story, the more they impact your life in either a positive or negative way. Ultimately each of us has a choice in how and who we want to be. This highlights why, in addition to being aware of your children's needs, it's important to be mindful of your own needs and behaviours and how they influence and impact your children.

Life is full of uncertainties and even more so when it comes to children. They are often unpredictable and there are times when you may wonder where they came from and what to do! How you navigate each of these basic human needs and how you guide your children to manage them will make a difference in how they thrive in life.

If you reflect on the six basic human needs, each has an opposing side. If you take, for example, the seeking of certainty, where there is certainty there is also uncertainty; where there is happiness, there is also sadness; where there is significance there is also insignificance in each and every one of us. One can't exist without the other.

When we accept the notion that a desire for something can't exist without an opposite, we find equilibrium – or what could be described as ultimate happiness. In other words, when going through everyday life, riding the waves of parenting and the unpredictable nature of life, when you are able to acknowledge that every experience is teaching you something, you are able to let go of any attachment to whether it is good or bad, happy or sad, successful or unsuccessful. You then become more conscious and aware of how you respond to whatever life is serving you and start to be consciously or fully aware of how you view and respond to each experience through thoughts, your emotions and actions.

Every human response to the opposites that occur are connected to what Demartini (2022) refers to as the 3i's:

- **Impulsive** responses or reactions
- **Instinctive** responses or reactions
- **Intuitive** responses or reactions.

Each of these responses are controlled by the brain and refers to how you react to circumstances or to each of the needs or desires you wish to fulfill. What does this have to do with parenting your child through their education? Learning how to respond to changes in relationships, transitions, social issues, financial and time stresses, particularly throughout your children's education, helps you to navigate the journey in a way that is conscious, and purposeful. The more aware you are of yourself and your children at a deeper level and how you respond to each situation, provides you with a renewed sense of stability and centredness.

Reflecting on your own life story can assist you to create a vision for how you would like to create connections with yourself and your child. This provides a first step towards managing yourself, your responsibilities, and your responses to anything that happens throughout your journey with your children, as you inspire them to thrive their learning.

What is your story?

This activity can be helpful to reflect on your life experiences, milestones and life events that have shaped who you are. This will help you to reflect on the influences in your life, how they have shaped your values and beliefs, what your education was like and how it could influence your choices and decisions when it comes to your child's education. Once you have reflected and learned more about your own journey, you can then share appropriate stories with your children about your life to encourage them as they navigate learning at school, at home and in the community.

Using a journal or sheet of paper, follow the steps to identify key moments in your life that provided you with lessons that form your identity as a person and as a parent.

Step 1

Draw a timeline of experiences that have shaped you over your lifetime in periods of seven to ten years from birth up to the age you are currently. Write down your significant moments on your timeline. Describe each experience. How did these experiences enable you to grow as a person? Would you classify them as positive or negative experiences at that time? Can you look at each of them as lessons that taught you something or that allowed you to grow? How do you view them now?

Step 2

Using the knowledge you have gained from those experiences, how were you able to move through each significant event? What was it that gave you the strength to overcome challenges or setbacks?

How did these experiences shape who you are today? Would you change anything about the choices you made or the experiences you had? What would you do differently? What did you learn about yourself and others through each experience?

Step 3

How can you use what you learned to guide and support your child through their learning process? Are you prepared to view the challenging experiences they have as opportunities for them to learn?

What were the things that you enjoyed or that made you happy?

What lessons can you share with your children to help them make positive choices based on your own experiences or those that you witnessed?

What stories can you share that can provide them with seeds of advice that may help them to navigate their path?

The opportunity to reflect on yourself is so important to your journey as a person and as a parent. The role of raising children is different for everyone because everyone brings different life experiences to the unique relationship between parent and child.

The experiences you have had in the past can shape the person you are today. However, young people are not always shown that they have a choice in who they want to be. In my own upbringing, I wasn't taught that self care, self love and self worth are such critical elements that need to be constantly nurtured so that we are able to care for others. The way you treat yourself is the most important part of this life journey and one that often takes a back seat. It is when you stop to self reflect, to learn to see yourself through a different lens and to create positive habits that can bring happiness, that you see the impact of this on your children.

There are many expectations on parents to get it right, to know what to do and how to raise children, but it is a journey of self discovery and an identity and path that only you can create. In the next chapter we will explore what that identity means for you so you can dive deeper into who you want to be as a parent, particularly as your children move through each transition and you enable yourself to grow alongside them.

Chapter 2

IDENTITY

When I discover who I am, I'll be free.

MOHAMMED ALI

The "parent" identity

In this lifelong journey of discovery, it is a beneficial process to uncover who you are, what you stand for and what you believe in. Who do you aspire to be and who are you now compared to who you were raised to believe you are. Exploring your identity can help you better understand who you are now and how you are impacting your own life and the people around you. Your deep knowledge of yourself can influence the type of people your children will become, as they are reflections of you and other influences around them.

Once you have had a chance to explore your identity, you will have a deeper understanding of yourself and what you might like to or not pass on to your children. We will explore specifically what those qualities are by discovering your identity through two main areas:

- Your vision
- Your values

As I have continued to grow and learn in my role as a parent of school-aged and now adult children, I realised the need to be more conscious of who I am and what I demonstrate to my children. I became more aware of the fact that each of the individual people I am raising is unique; even though they have inherited similar traits to myself, including family habits, values and genetics, they are ultimately their own person, here to forge their own path. With this in mind, I am fully aware of raising them as individuals with their own minds, personalities, values and attitudes. Your children, with you as their guide, should have the opportunity to grow confidently and have conviction in their ideas, passions and the pathways they choose.

To explore this further, let's consider "parent" as an identity. As a parent you have the opportunity to discover your own identity and ways to raise your children. There seems to be enormous pressure on parents today – in how they approach raising their children; what to do and what not to do; how to look; and a constant narrative around what they are doing wrong rather than what they are achieving. The wonderful part of the role of parent is that it is a constant journey of discovery and there is no perfect way to parent. How you parent may not always suit the mainstream narrative or conform to what others expect from you. You have a choice in how you wish to raise your children.

> Choice is the most powerful tool we have.
> Everything boils down to choice.
> We exist in a field of infinite possibilities.
> Every choice we make shuts an infinite number of doors
> and opens an infinite number of doors.
> At any point we can change the direction of our lives
> by a simple choice.
> It is all in our hands, our hearts, our minds.
>
> UNKNOWN

As one of the most important influencers in your child's life, you are on a journey to support them to learn from a range of experiences so they are able to thrive and manage themselves in their everyday life.

Knowing what your identity as a parent is or what it could be begins by understanding your actual role as parent. For most of us, the roles have been demonstrated and influenced by our own parents and their parents before them. For women, the role of mother has traditionally been considered as "nurturer". For men, the role of father has historically been viewed as "protector" or "provider". But society has shifted away from such fixed roles, enabling any or all parents and carers to nurture, protect and provide for their children.

One of the most common responsibilities for many parents to fulfil is the need to prepare their children to eventually leave the nest. The role of parent is that of supporter and guide to help children get to the point where they have the strength, courage, skills and confidence to take that leap – it also includes supporting their education and aspirations, and guiding them on the path towards achieving those aspirations. In a world that is constantly changing and increasingly competitive, with opportunities for multiple professions, but also an increase in populations across the globe, how can you, as their main influencer, supporter and guide, prepare and inspire your children? In reflecting on this, it is easy to fall into the trap of fear. Fear of the future, fear for your children, fear of the world they are entering and how your child will cope in such a competitive and uncertain environment.

One of the ways you can guide your children is through demonstrating your work ethic and attitudes towards relationships, mental health and wellbeing, lifestyle, work, and money. Parents' attitudes often influence children's views about all these aspects of life. In Ellen Galinsky's book *Ask The Children* (2000) – an exploration of children's opinions on various topics – she asked children what their views were on their parents working. "First, we tend to hold parents responsible for all the problems children face ... Those children wouldn't have problems if it weren't for their parents. When fingers are pointed at parents for causing children's problems, working mothers are often singled out ...". There is a problem, but the problem is not the fact that mothers or fathers work. The problem is that jobs themselves can be stressful or satisfying. Jobs can drain us or energise us. Jobs can overwhelm us or support us. The problem is how we work and how this impacts family life.

You can make choices to be intentional in how you bring your work life into the home, how you show children that work is a part of your life, and what that means for your family.

During the pandemic your children may have had the opportunity to see you at work in the home. They may have seen another side to you and witnessed your work ethic, attitudes to work, and whether your job drains or energises you. This may not have happened without the opportunity to work from home, which offered a chance to demonstrate how the world of work actually looks, albeit slightly different to previous times. For many, it was a unique learning experience for the whole family.

My own children have watched me working from home since they were born, so they know that work can be satisfying and rewarding, but also challenging. Your role is to be mindful of the impressions you are leaving on your children when it comes to views about work, money, and how you live life as a family. They are always watching and learning from you. If you are dissatisfied or stressed in your job, how can you create some positive changes? Are there opportunities to find a balance between work and family life, to enjoy both and to provide your children with positive attitudes and ethics when it comes to working? How can you demonstrate problem solving when there are stresses at work, show your children how to manage in a crisis, and model the importance of work-life balance?

Understanding the bigger picture role of parenting

Dr Lea Waters, author of *The Strength Switch* (2000), talks about parents as being 24/7 CEOs of our kids' lives. Your role as the CEO is to be "responsible for all the different departments: cognitive, physical, social, emotional, moral, sexual, spiritual, cultural, and educational. The buck starts and stops with us".

When it comes to defining a parent identity, perhaps you could think of yourself as the CEO of your home. What is the bigger picture you are seeking as the creator of your own role as a parent?

A successful CEO manages the people they lead with openness, guidance, understanding, empathy and compassion. They give their staff the freedom to grow as people, focusing on the strengths of each person and nurturing the areas that need further guidance. A CEO doesn't own the people, they are the steward of the people. As CEO of your home, you are the leader, managing various aspects of the home and guiding the family towards a shared vision, while also supporting each individual's vision for their own life. As the leader in your home, you share the responsibility of influencing, nurturing and caring for your children with your village – which may consist of your partner, extended family, friends and/or educators.

It's important to understand that being CEO is not about having power and control over others, it's about having a clear understanding and awareness of your role and responsibilities as a parent, and what this means on a daily basis. It's about understanding what you can and can't control, focusing on what is within your ability to manage, such as setting boundaries and co-designing family rules. It is about knowing when to let go and little by little allow your children to become more self-sufficient and independent, especially when it comes to their learning, growth and education.

Children only spend a short time of their lives with us, and it's easy to want to hold onto them for as long as possible. But claiming ownership over children, while fulfilling the desire for certainty, can lead to craving control over everything they do and experience, and can result in impeding your child's growth. Instead, as CEO of the home, you can support them to create the life they want, to develop the courage and confidence to move forward into each new experience, and to live life on their terms as they mature. It's a fine balance between providing the foundational skills, managing the different milestones, and letting go as each one unfolds, setting the boundaries they need and nurturing them to be their own unique selves. We'll explore this further when we look at Transitions in Chapter 3.

There are many examples of successful people who attribute their achievements to the support of their families. Often it was their parents who recognised their strengths and interests and nurtured them towards achieving their greatest potential. People like Elon Musk, Sir Richard Branson, Serena and Venus Williams, Ash Barty, Tiger Woods, Roger Federer, and many more, attribute much of their success to the guidance and support of their parents and extended family.

As CEO of your home, you can observe the strengths in your child and are able to identify ways that you can support them in their aspirations and dreams. Dreams can be reached when you have a vision and work out a plan of action to work towards achieving it.

Vision

A great CEO, leader or elite athlete has a vision and plan for the path they are taking. They plan and implement the actions they need to be able to achieve their goals. They have contingency plans to manage uncertainty and to reduce and navigate risks and challenges that arise when things don't go to plan. They have a broader, birds-eye view of the landscape and can see what is up ahead. All this begins with a vision.

A vision can provide you with something to aim for. Instead of floundering or bouncing around each day, treading water or drowning in uncertainties. A vision helps you focus, plan ahead and manage yourself. It can help you avoid feeling overwhelmed or anxious when things seem out of control.

To create your vision, let's begin by exploring and reflecting on what you imagine your parenting journey will look like, from the time your child is very young, through their schooling and into their adult life. It can be helpful to encourage your partner or your child's other caregiver/s to also write down their vision, then discuss it together. This will help you understand what each of you are aiming for with each of your children. Bear in mind that your vision may need to be flexible as you get to know your child or children because they will each be different. Your partner's vision may also be different but this gives you a chance to discuss each of your views together and come to agreements without adversely impacting your child.

1. Create a vision map

You may like to map out your parenting journey by your child's age (every seven years) as you did with your self reflection in Chapter 1.

A vision is your reason, or your "why". It is the bigger picture of what you desire to achieve. In preparing your vision, it's important to remember that, as mentioned earlier, life is full of uncertainties so you will need to be flexible. Your vision may not be fulfilled to each minute detail but it is a pathway that you can create to guide you on the journey.

> **Here are some questions you may like to consider when creating your vision:**
>
> - What are your hopes for your children at each of their milestones when it comes to their academic and social/emotional growth?
> - What is your specific role in the life of your child? What does this look like for you and, more importantly, how will your role impact the child?
> - Why is your role in their life important to consider?
> - What does it mean to be a role model for your child? Why is this important?

- What habits do you have that you may not want your child to inherit?
- What values do you feel are important to impart with your children? How can you demonstrate these values through your actions?
- How will you be present and mindful at each stage of your child's growth and development? Why is this important to you? Why is it important for your child?
- What expectations do you have for them as individuals and as learners, both at home and at school? Where do these expectations come from? Why are you setting these expectations for your child? Are you willing to be flexible if your child doesn't meet your expectations?
- What are your greatest hopes for your child as they journey through school and through life?
- How will you guide and support them to forge their own path?
- If you are seeking happiness for your child, what does that look like for them?
- How will you manage your own emotions if your child is not happy or has setbacks?
- What was your experience at school like? How does this impact your vision for your child or each of your children? What would you like to see for them that is different to your own experience?

Take your time to answer these questions. There are no right or wrong answers as they come from within you and your own experiences. The questions are designed to help you reflect on your own personal views and feelings, to help you uncover and visualise where you feel your journey will take you. You can use a journal to track your progress, express your thoughts, share what you are feeling along the way and record how you respond as each of your child's milestones occurs. Remember to celebrate wins and keep improving yourself, as a person and in your role as parent. Self reflection is a form of therapy and when you write your vision down, you'll start to see the person you want to be within the vision you have for your children.

2. Reflect on your identity as a parent

Take some time to reflect on how you view yourself in your identity as a parent. Here are a few questions to answer in a journal or on a notepad to reflect on who you are now and to establish the identity or values you wish to have as you guide your child through their learning.

- How would you currently describe yourself as a parent?
- Do you feel a sense of protection or ownership of your children, or do you see yourself as enabling your children to grow and become independent?
- What qualities and values do you believe you bring to this unique role?
- Is there anything you feel you need to change? Why?
- What do you love about being a parent? Why?
- What do you believe you have learned from your own parents or other role models that you would like to pass onto your children? What have you consciously avoided bringing to your parenting style? Why?
- What motivates you to be a good parent? What does a good parent look like for you? Why?
- Who is the parent you aspire to be?
- Do you have any role models you aspire to emulate or do you have your own vision of how a parent should be?
- What qualities do your role models have that you can learn from? What qualities and strengths do you already have that will help you to be like that person? What are you doing each day to become like that person?
- What intentions can you set for yourself each day to help you become the person you want to be in the role of parent?
- How do you typically manage yourself when things are difficult or challenging?
- How do you make the most of the time you have with your children?

- What were your expectations or perceptions of what parenting your child through their education would be like? Have those expectations been met for you, or has your experience been completely different to what you expected? What might you change and why?

Take your time to answer the questions I've posed, using them as a guide to reflect on your why. You can then write a short vision statement for you and your child; what your hopes and dreams are for them as they move through their early development and formative years, and how you hope to influence, inspire, guide and support them along the way. Ask them also what their hopes and dreams are for their learning. Ask what inspires them to learn, so you can understand their needs.

Take some time to reflect on each question and particularly on your own childhood experiences at school. If you feel that reflecting on past experiences brings on anxieties or triggers you in any way, perhaps talking with a professional may assist in understanding what those triggers are and how to manage them. Consider the aspects of your education you would want your child to experience, bearing in mind that this is their unique journey and they may not experience their education the same way you did. Their journey is a blank page that is waiting to be filled with their own unique stories and experiences, with your support and guidance.

Once you have reflected on the questions above, an example of a vision might be:

> My vision as a parent is to encourage, guide and support my children to make good choices and to be kind and compassionate individuals who care for others. My vision is to be present when they need me, to actively listen to them, to ask them questions, to hear their answers and encourage them to develop as unique individuals with their own strengths and interests. My vision is to surround them with good influences, to guide them towards positive relationships by demonstrating this within our family and friendship circle and to provide many learning opportunities that strengthen them as people and as inspired, lifelong learners.

I encourage you to write your own vision in your own words and to continue to revisit it as your children grow. As you move through this book, you may wish to revise your vision as you learn more about your role. Remember to stay true to the vision for yourself and your children, it's about you being present as a parent and understanding your role in supporting your children to reach their potential and achieve their dreams.

Values

When considering how you will guide and support your children on their learning journey, one major area to explore is your values. Demartini (2020) states, "Your values determine how you perceive the world, what actions you take (or don't take), and what you ultimately achieve in your life … Unless you genuinely value something, you won't persevere … Your values drive your purpose."

Each of us is driven by our values; whether we are aware of it or not, we live our values each day. Values often stem from our own upbringing, culture or experiences – including what we've learned from various influences as children. When we enter into a partnership with another person, we each bring values that may differ, or that are similar, into the relationship and into the family.

Values play an important role in how we choose partners, friends, and careers. When it comes time to choose a school, values can play a large role in the final choice. Values lead to the decisions we make, that then lead to actions and eventually to results. You can understand how values impact the way you parent your child through their education by understanding what exactly your values are and how they affect your decisions, perceptions, actions and results.

In your daily life, your values are linked to how you treat yourself and others, the foods you cook and eat, the places you visit, the content you consume, how much exercise you do, how you communicate with others, the people you surround yourself with, and your lifestyle and career choices. Yet most of us may not know or haven't been taught the importance of reflecting on the many decisions we make in relation to our values.

When you become more aware of your values and how they impact your life, you are able to be more conscious and purposeful about your choices, particularly when it comes to your role as a parent.

When it comes to values in parenting, especially when your child begins school, some issues can arise such as:

- Creating unrealistic expectations
- Aligning yourself to others' values instead of your own
- Forming perceptions that cloud your judgment
- Reacting or responding impulsively to things that impact your child
- Fearing what could go wrong instead of noticing what is going right or what lessons are being learned when challenges arise.

Great expectations

> It takes guts to be accepting of who your child is,
> to be at peace, to let go.
>
> AUSTEJA LANDSBERGIENE (2018)

As a parent, perhaps one of your highest values is that you want the best for your children. This can lead to developing various levels of expectations – either for ourselves, for teachers or for children – that may not always be realistic or achievable. You may have even set certain expectations while writing your vision, which is ok. The exercise is designed to help you to think about your expectations and how you manage what comes along with them.

Touching again on the expectation of happiness, ask yourself if it is realistic to expect children to be happy all of the time at school, or to always achieve academic excellence. This may be one of your highest values, but it is worthwhile considering if extremely high expectations of happiness and academic success will actually make them happy or successful.

If you value the happiness of your children, and no doubt you do, what exactly does this look like for them? Does this mean that you focus only on your children being satisfied all the time? What lengths will you go to in order to maintain that happiness? What if everything must go their way in order for them to be happy? If that's the case, how will they manage when they are faced with sadness or dealing with grief or loss – these are opposite emotions that they need to learn how to manage, with your guidance.

Think for a moment also about what it means for you when your child is happy. Do you secretly want this so that your life is easier? Yes, you can admit this, especially if this is one of your highest values. It's a secret (or not-so-secret) wish for most people. When children are happy, our lives are actually easier. There are fewer challenges to navigate, less meltdowns, less stress, and life can be a breeze! So there's nothing wrong with wanting them to be happy. But children are not going to be happy all the time. They are going to have many emotions and all kinds of challenges. They will express themselves differently at different stages, but they will still need your support to navigate their early lives, teenage years and adulthood.

Consider these values in relation to your child's education:

- **Excellent academic achievement** – if you value academic achievement, what does this mean for how your children approach their learning, their attitude, motivation and aspirations?
- **Growth** – Will you focus on how they are growing in their learning and as a whole person rather than just their academic results? Will growth be a high value?
- **Future success** – If future success is a high value, what does that look like for your child?
- **Enabling opportunities** – are you willing to actively participate in providing other learning opportunities to enhance your children's learning, growth and future prospects?
- **External support** – if academic excellence is a high value, will your children have to study harder, have extra tutoring outside of school and put in extra study hours to achieve high grades? How will this benefit them? Are there other ways you can support them to achieve their full potential? Are there other external influences and role models you can surround them with to enhance their learning and opportunities?

How will you respond or react (using the 3i's discussed earlier) if they don't achieve a "successful education" according to your values?

Sometimes we forget that children are still learning and that they learn at different paces to each other. Observing your children and how they are different is important when reflecting on the values and expectations you have for your child's education. Are you prepared to acknowledge that although your values may be well intentioned, you may need a level of flexibility? Your values may not always mean that your children can reach your expectations.

While it is helpful to reflect on and understand your vision and values when it comes to your child's education and learning, flexibility in setting expectations is required for you to fulfill your role in guiding and supporting your child. Having expectations and encouraging your children to achieve can be positive and can enable your child to feel they are capable. However, be mindful that your expectations don't get to a point where the end result is more important than nurturing your child's growth, in alignment with their strengths and abilities.

I'm sharing this with you so you are prepared for those times when your children come home and are not happy or have not had the best day, or perhaps when they don't receive the grade or results you might expect. In recent years, there has been more focus in the school curriculum on the wellbeing of children, with increased funding of wellbeing programs and the development of national wellbeing frameworks. I experienced the benefits of this during my children's time in their primary years, with the school adopting the Kidsmatter Framework and several wellbeing programs. These programs provide the grounding and skills children need to understand and improve their social and emotional wellbeing, as the research indicates this impacts their academic learning. More recently, in October 2018, the national Australian Student Wellbeing Framework was introduced to ensure a focus on helping children to manage personal and social capabilities of self management, self awareness, social management and social awareness. These are qualities you can support your children with at home; what they are learning in school about each of these can be demonstrated and practiced at home (ACARA 2023). This may require you to be more informed about what they are learning so you can implement the strategies at home, use consistent language and terminology and demonstrate to your child that you are supporting their wellbeing.

As the adults who surround children, we need to work together to prepare children for the realities of life. In other words, as we have explored, there are good times and there are the opposite – there is certainty and uncertainty. These dualities are a factor in everyone's life and it's important that you demonstrate how to manage these ups and downs so that children also learn these important life skills.

It's also essential to celebrate wins and successes, no matter how small or big. Every step we take in life is one step closer to achieving what we want, and the journey can be more rewarding than the outcome. The success equation, according to billionaire Dr Kazuo Inamori (2022) is:

$$\text{Attitude} \times \text{Effort} \times \text{Ability} = \text{Success}$$

Success as a value or aspiration is different for everyone (Harvey 2023). Depending on your definition of success, you may wish to support your child to master the three elements of attitude, effort and ability to help them reach their potential. Attitude goes a long way to foster the motivation required to put in the effort. All three relate to the cognitive and non-cognitive skills needed for learning, which we will explore in Chapter 8. Remember that it takes patience to master new abilities, and effort and attitude are essential to bring it all together.

My niece is an Olympic taekwondo athlete and has experienced all of these elements. With the right attitude, effort and ability, she has been able to achieve most of her goals so far. In addition to her success and accolades, her experiences have seen her grow in confidence as a person. She has learned that it takes time, effort, dedication and perseverance to reach the point of the final goal.

At her first Olympics, my niece was tested beyond belief. She was competing during the pandemic so there were no people in the audience at her fight. Her family were unable to attend to support her. Despite making the most of the experience, learning more about how to improve, learning from other athletes and discovering more about herself and what she was capable of, she was beaten in the first round. When she returned home, she had to be isolated for two weeks before she could see her family – who had been supporting her every step of the way. After finally reaching the Olympics, it was a very lonely experience. Her strength during this time was truly tested and it was this strength, along with her attitude, that inspired her to keep going, to continue dreaming, training and reaching for the next goal. Even when people do reach their goals, there is always something else needed to stay focused and remain at the top of their game.

Over the past twenty years I have admired and observed one of the greatest tennis players of all time, Roger Federer. He would practice every day so that he could maintain his strength, skills and fitness. He did whatever it took to maintain a level that was at the pinnacle of his sport. It would have taken hard work, patience, perseverance and determination not to give up. His attitude and effort are admired by many fans around the world and by other players who respect his integrity. His skills and ability are exceptional, but his attitude won many fans. These were the ingredients for his ultimate success and victories. No matter how many trophies sit in his cabinet, he knows what it took to earn them. It wasn't just about the end result but the journey along the way and the people who surrounded him that provided the support he needed to keep going.

The values instilled in both of these athletes were likely formed within them as young children. Perhaps their parents had high expectations or aspirations for them and encouraged them to have dreams and achieve them. Each experience you have in life presents you with an opportunity to learn a lesson, to anticipate what is to come, to examine what you need to work on or consider which direction to take next. Your role in supporting and guiding your children is to focus on how you will provide them with opportunities to grow as people and in strengthening their skills so they are able to achieve their full potential. Your expectations must be realistic and aligned with what they want to achieve or what they are capable of achieving, so you are then able to provide them with the support they need.

Aligning with your values

When it comes to understanding your own values and how you demonstrate these for your children, it's helpful to explore how you manage yourself when other people's values don't align with your own. It's very possible that your child's values may differ from yours at some stage during their growth. You may also encounter challenges if teachers or other parents you meet through the school experience have values that differ from yours.

When faced with this possibility, it's helpful to refer back to Anthony Robbins' six core needs (discussed in Chapter 1). We can also consider Maslow's hierarchy of human needs – one of which is acceptance or belonging (Abulof 2017). Schools are very much a place where children seek a sense of belonging, in friendship groups and in where they fit in the classroom. But it's not only children who experience this – I recall my own experiences when my first child began school. I felt triggered as I entered the school environment for the first time as an adult. It felt as if I was back at school myself, having to make new friends and find a tribe in this new environment to feel that sense of belonging.

When I first stepped into the school yard again, I felt as though the culture of parents was very similar to the students when I was at school. There were various groups of people who gravitate towards each other – they may have had shared interests or values. This created a culture of separate groups. As I navigated my way through these groups to see whether I fit in, I found the talk and behaviour amongst some parents could sometimes be quite judgemental and out of alignment with my values. Initially I felt unsafe again; I felt that I would have to work hard to fit in, much like I had felt at school – which sometimes meant going against my family values. This presented a challenge for me as I was actually dealing with a memory rather than a reality. I was no longer at school but feelings were still appearing in my subconscious. I needed to really reflect on my personal values and how they aligned with other people I was meeting. I had to consider how I could still remain true to my values and impart them to my children without feeling pressured to conform or fit in with other people's expectations. You may notice everything I refer to here relates back to how we feel. Feelings have an impact on how we respond and how we know when something is out of alignment with our values. If you feel uncomfortable or that you don't fit in with how others' speak or behave, you need to check in with yourself to either overcome these triggers and emotions and not let them affect you, or align yourself with people who are similar to you.

This kick started my interest in wanting to understand more about human behaviour and what actually causes parents to behave a certain way in the school environment. I was curious about how people parent their children through their education, and what the parent role is when we return to that environment as adults. With so many different parenting styles and values related to what parents allow their children to do or how they behave, it looked to me like a very complex culture that needed to be explored further to understand how to create an environment for parents that was welcoming and inclusive, that didn't trigger or exacerbate past emotional trauma.

Developing the culture of a school environment is not only the responsibility of the staff and students. It can be heavily influenced by the parents in the community and the environment they create for the children. Children are watching and learning from us all the time, particularly how we interact in our friendship circles and relationships with other adults.

Think about a time when you may have inadvertently, or perhaps reluctantly, aligned with others' values and beliefs and completely ignored your own? Perhaps you were in a social situation such as the school environment, where you were with a group of people who were talking about another person in a negative way. If one of your values is respect and compassion for others, how would this discussion sit with you? Would you participate to fit into that social setting, or would you decline to participate in such a discussion?

Think about that or another time and reflect on which, if any, of your values were out of alignment. How did this impact your decisions, responses and the outcome of that conversation or situation? Did you feel pressured to conform to other people's expectations, or did you stick to your own values and speak up about the conversation that was unfolding?

If you fall into the trap of aligning yourself with other people's values when it comes to parenting and your children's education, you may need to reflect on whether you are being true to your authentic self. If you feel the need to align with others' values to fit in, particularly in a school environment, it quickly becomes a game you can't win and you yourself will feel unhappy if you are not honouring your own values.

This can happen within other relationships with friends or family, when other people have certain values and expectations that we don't agree with or that don't match ours. If you truly know what your values are, it is easier to stay true to yourself while also being open and flexible in how you view others' values and beliefs. You don't need to take on others' values but you can acknowledge them as different to yours and still stay true to your own values.

Finding a balance between staying true to your values and accepting others' values as different to yours gives you a clearer perspective when deciding who you choose to associate with. This can hold true when it comes to making new friends in the school environment and when considering who you want your children to be influenced by. You can't expect people to change for you, but you have a choice as to whether you want to be a part of that circle or not. You can lead by example and show others' how to behave more positively, to create a cultural shift. This can then provide a more caring and compassionate environment for children to be influenced by rather than any toxic behaviour impacting their learning.

An example I can share with you relates to a misalignment of values with a sporting club. My daughter was playing soccer for a local club and although the team was going well and the children were well behaved and enjoying learning the game, some of the parents in the club were not so well behaved. The culture of the club was out of alignment with my values and the people were not who I wanted to surround my children with, so I made the decision to change clubs. Instead of being influenced by other people's values in this instance, I was able to reflect on my own values and make necessary changes. This ensured my child was able to have more positive influences around her while she continued to grow in her sport. I spoke with my child about the decision to move, as this was an important learning opportunity for her to understand how to remain in alignment with herself and her values.

You have a choice in this kind of situation – you can be mindful and tolerant of organisational cultures or behaviours that don't align with your values; you can try to change the culture, although this is unlikely to happen quickly; or you can remove yourself from what doesn't feel right for you. Your relationship with yourself is one of the most important to nurture, and is key to developing a stronger understanding of your own values, expectations, relationships and connections with your children and others in your family and community. These are discussions you can also have with your children about how to manage in these situations.

I have witnessed parents making judgements or forming a perception of a teacher before even getting to know them, perhaps based on their own views of what an ideal teacher should be for their child. This type of behaviour inspired me to work towards creating cultural shifts in school communities, starting with my children's school. This was the beginning of a new career for me, which I didn't see coming. I began with researching parent and teacher views about their relationship and what impact this has on students. One of the questions I asked teachers was, "What relational skills do you feel you need to be able to build relationships and gain confidence with parents?"

One response was, "I think it is important to be an open and transparent person. It is important that your values are on display to the people you work with and that these values are lived, not just said."

I also posed the question, "Do you sometimes feel judged by parents?"

One response was, "I'm sure there are times when my actions and decisions are being judged by parents. After all, I am in charge of a whole year's education of the person they made! I never do anything I can't justify, so I am confident in my teaching practice that I am making good decisions about the direction of my students."

Some teachers are more than willing to develop a partnership approach with parents. However, they need to feel that you are a willing partner also. They, too, need to stay true to their values while also acknowledging and embracing the values of others, all while preserving this special relationship between teacher and parent to help the student succeed. We will explore the special relationship between parents and teachers in Chapter 4.

When people are judgemental, rude towards others or gossip about teachers, it may not be deliberately malicious. This behaviour can stem from past triggers or trauma, uncertainty or misinformation, or a lack of awareness of how to deal with challenges that arise. This can result in impulsive behaviour such as showing anger or misjudgement of the situation or person. People who feel like they are not being heard or are not receiving answers, may become critical, or their behaviour may be based on a perception they have formed. The teacher I interviewed for my research admitted that "... any judgements that are made usually come from a misinformed point of view, so it's more likely my responsibility to better inform parents."

What are the values you currently have or can create within your family that demonstrate respect and courtesy and being mindful of how you respond to challenges? You might like to list these in your journal.

Some examples of family values might be:

- **Respect** – showing courtesy and thinking of others in the family and how you treat them.
- **Mindfulness** – being mindful of others before making too much noise; not interrupting when someone is speaking. Being aware of how you speak to people and avoiding gossip or speaking unkindly about others.
- **Positive communication** – communicating with respect using positive language.

- **Thoughtfulness** – if feelings and emotions escalate, taking time to breathe and think before speaking; trying not to act on impulse or misinterpretations.
- **Helping each other** – asking for help or asking others if they need help.
- **Quality time** – eating meals together and spending quality time together.
- **Traditions or rituals** – creating family traditions that provide a sense of belonging and connection.
- **Inclusiveness** – demonstrating respect for each other even if we are different.
- **Feedback** – providing constructive feedback rather than criticism.

Feel free to add more to this list in your journal.

The values that you demonstrate will directly impact how your children behave, how they treat others and, most importantly, how they view themselves.

What values can you demonstrate that support your child's education?

Some examples of values for your child's education are:

- **Positivity** – encouraging your child to focus on effort and a positive attitude towards their learning.
- **Love** – creating a space and culture at home that fosters a love for learning and of self.
- **Awareness** – checking in with your child regularly to see how they are managing friendships and their learning. Stay in touch with their social development and provide support.
- **Mindfulness** – actively listening to understand any challenges; not reacting immediately or impulsively to anything they share but instead being mindful in your response.
- **Support** – advocating on behalf of your child in a positive way; working alongside the teacher as a partner by sharing any challenges or questions your child may have without the temptation to blame or project anger towards the teacher or the school.

- **Openness** – asking questions of your child to support their learning and enabling them to find the answers, keeping in mind they are still learning.
- **Kindness** – being kind to yourself, your child and their teachers if they don't have all the answers. Exploring the answers together.
- **Respect** – communicating with teachers in a respectful way, recognising that, as professionals, they can provide support but that you also have a role to play at home.

Writing down your own personal and family values may form part of your vision statement or you may wish to keep them separate and add to them as you come across different situations you need to navigate or respond to. Thinking about your values and writing them down will help you determine what is important to you when it comes to your family life and your child's education and how you might support their learning and development. These are the values you wish to align with and live by, leading by example for your children while also staying true to your authentic self.

Your identity as parent is constantly being shaped and tweaked as you learn to navigate the various experiences you encounter. You don't need to have all the answers, but use the approach of learning as you go and discovering what works for you and your children.

Now that you have explored your vision for your role in your child's learning, as well as your values and how you would like to incorporate these into the journey, you have the roadmap to follow and guide you along the way. You will now be more aware of signposts that are giving you directions in how you want to guide your child as they make their way through their formal education. We will explore further aspects of your role in more detail in Chapter 5, Roles and responsibilities. In the next chapter we will explore how you can manage the numerous transitions and changes your child will go through over their time at school and how you can learn to create connections while also letting go to enable them to grow.

Chapter 3
TRANSITIONS

*Life is change. Breathe in, breathe out. Smile, yawn, scowl.
Move, lie still. A multiplicity of changes takes place at all times
in your body; digestion, respiration, circulation.
Growth pushes you up and out, aging mellows you.
The possibility of changing yourself is always there.*

ALISON HAYNES 2004

Change is happening constantly to each of us, even if we are not always consciously aware of it. Change is something you either embrace or resist; how you perceive and react to it can determine your overall experience of it. When it comes to the changes and transitions your child goes through over time, the opportunity to embrace or resist is ever present – you can influence how you react and respond to these changes through the stories you tell yourself.

As your children move through each stage of their life journey, you will be asked, forced or naturally know when it is time to let go of the various roles and responsibilities you have in their life. While your children are going through transitions and life changes, you are also going through these changes. If you are fully aware of the changes occurring in your life, as well as in the lives of your children, you are better able to support them and help them understand how to navigate the ebb and flow of life.

As I reflect on my own parenting, I recall how much I enjoyed being able to guide my children and witness them achieve many milestones when they were younger. As they grew and made their way through each stage of growth, even though I was proud of how far they'd come, I sometimes felt a sense of sadness as they no longer needed as much of my support. As I reflect on it now, I believe I went through periods of mourning as each transition passed. This, I realised, was part of my own growth as a person. The special role I have continues today, as I guide them to that next level of learning and maturity, to have a sense of themselves, to achieve more independence, and to move confidently into their next phase.

With each transition, my role needed to shift slightly as I navigated the new person they were becoming. This is what I'd like to explore with you, to support you in your role as a constant navigator of change and the master of your own self growth.

Each learning stage for your children is an opportunity for you to be available to guide and support them, to observe their learning and development and to remain an integral part of their journey. Each transition is a time to regroup, reflect and understand your new role as parent alongside your child as they navigate change. Perhaps revisit your vision and try to recognise that this is a normal part of the parenting journey, then factor into your vision how you can manage yourself and your emotions through each transitional stage.

> Sometimes you never know the value of a moment
> until it becomes a memory.
>
> DR SEUSS

As much as it can sometimes seem like groundhog day when children are babies, they are learning so much and there are so many changes occurring. I love the above quote by Dr Seuss, as it really focuses on the importance of being in the moment with your children and being fully aware of their development at every stage. It may be tempting to want them to reach the next stage or milestone quickly, as life is so fast paced. Developing an appreciation for the growth and learning happening before your eyes, for your child, and for yourself, is a profound experience. It can provide you with many opportunities to know your children and yourself at a deeper level.

I think I may have intuitively known about being present and in the moment when my children were younger, but I had very little knowledge of the science behind how they were learning. Being fully aware and mindful or in the moment wasn't as much of a trend then as it is now. I really didn't know that it was so important and only discovered this while learning to become a coach, trainer and facilitator. This was reinforced when writing my first book, as I explored research into the different ways that children learn, and the way the brain works and determines how we respond to changes.

The Theory of Development by Jerome Bruner states that

> when children are born, they are already learning and are ready to learn. They have a natural and instinctive curiosity and are actively learning from birth without being consciously aware of it. The purpose of education is not to impart knowledge, but instead to facilitate a child's thinking and problem-solving skills which can then be transferred to a range of situations. (Levitas & Hurst 2021).

Even though children are natural learners, they need your guidance to understand their learning, to enhance their learning experiences and to encourage their wonderful, natural curiosity. As they begin to experiment, take risks and transition to their next phase of life, you may feel the desire to resist these changes and even unintentionally hold them back. Your responses to how they are learning, interacting with new experiences and how they are changing, are an important part of their development – they will constantly seek signals and guidance from you so your awareness is critical to their learning.

The desire to hold them back may come from a fear of letting go and losing your connection with them, or a sense of "What is my role now?"

In exploring any fears or challenges in your role as your child moves through school, I'd like to expand on the six core needs that I touched on in Chapter 1. We can use these to explore how your values and beliefs impact how you can manage the changes that are constantly occurring in your life and your children's lives. As humans, we each have a value system that is connected to learned beliefs and desires for the following feelings or outcomes:

Certainty – clarity, control, balance, authority, success, superiority, power, freedom

Some people feel they need to have control over how things develop, or to seek the familiarity of what is commonly known as a comfort zone. As you navigate changes, you might seek the balance or freedom of the mind that certainty can provide. If you are seeking success for your child as they move through their learning journey, you might hold onto that need strongly because it provides you with a sense of certainty that they will be fine if they are successful. Certainty can provide a sense of security and power, and a balance within yourself when you know what is going to happen next.

Uncertainty – thrills, excitement, drama, unbalance, fear of failure, fear of success

Where there is certainty, there is also uncertainty. This can present as a feeling of being out of balance or not having control of situations and changes happening in your life or with your child. Some people find uncertainty thrilling and are comfortable with taking risks, others love the excitement and the drama of uncertainty as it keeps life interesting. Uncertainty can also trigger feelings of fear and frustration, which can be overwhelming and overpowering, especially when your children go through changes soon after you feel you have already mastered their previous changes.

Significance – the need to feel valued, belonging, appreciation, attention, importance, validation, superiority or elevating oneself

As a parent you may want to feel valued by your child. You want to feel that you are a significant part of their lives and they too, seek that in you. It's tempting to overcompensate in an attempt to feel valued by doing too many things for them. This might fulfil your need to be valued, but it can also prevent their growth. There will come a time when they can start doing things for themselves and when you need to set boundaries so they don't take advantage of your need to feel valued.

Some people seek validation from others to feel good about themselves. Others want to feel superior to feel significant and so they seek roles that elevate them to a certain status. These desires are also present for your children as they seek to be significant in your world as well as in their own friendship groups, class groups and teams. You may witness pecking orders develop as each person tries to seek significance within the group. Some may seek attention or want to be the boss, others may seek approval or validation; all are seeking significance in their pack or tribe.

In my own experience with my children and observing friendships and social behaviour, many children often seek significance – the need to be validated and to feel loved. While seeking significance is not new, it has certainly increased through social media channels as a mechanism for expressing or not receiving validity. In the past we may have sought significance in our small group of friends and family. Now it can be via strangers and a broader network of people who can provide this with an emoji, a "like", and other forms of validation on social media designed to fulfil that desire for significance and attention.

Variety – spontaneity, different experiences, rebellion

Many of us seek variety and experiences that provide something we haven't tried before. Children can be spontaneous in their approach to life, wanting to try new experiences and seek variety. Whether they are bored or just wanting to take a different approach, it's important to enable this, to encourage curiosity and experimentation (within reason) without the fear of uncertainty or failure. If their desire for variety goes unfulfilled, they may demonstrate rebellion to gain a feeling of control or to break out of boundaries you have set. This is a space to constantly navigate; you need to provide guidance with reasonable boundaries but also be flexible in enabling variety in their lives. When provided with a variety of experiences, children learn new ways of doing things and are not sheltered from the world around them. A variety of experiences assists their learning in so many ways as they are able to form connections in the brain and understand how to navigate different environments, people and opportunities.

Love/connection – belonging, feeling loved and cared for, worthy of love

No doubt the highest value for most humans is to be loved and feel worthy of love. The sense of belonging most of us crave is often a challenge – each of us is different and we don't always fit the mould or find others who understand us. Within a family, your child will be seeking a sense of connection, where they fit in the family in relation to siblings and how you connect with them. Home should be a place to feel safe, loved and cared for, and this is perhaps the greatest value of all to prioritise for children.

Growth – personal and professional growth, ambition, achievement, success

As your child moves through their formal education, you will see them grow and develop in their social, emotional and academic skills. Even though the structure of school curriculum and assessment determines the level your child can achieve, all children learn and grow at the pace they are able to. With your engagement, encouragement, support and guidance they can reach levels they are capable of reaching. Growth plays a major role in how they change along the way and is a necessary part of their learning.

Contribution – giving back to society, being a contributor in the family, in the workplace or in a team environment.

When we contribute our strengths to help others or to provide value, this value is often associated with giving back or being selfless and thinking of others. All the values that you desire and seek can be used as a way of motivating you to take action. It actually feels good when you are contributing. The feeling you receive from achieving your goals, or helping others is what motivates many people to make a difference in the world.

Children need love. As they grow older, they may begin to seek it through the *desire for significance* – looking for your attention in various ways, wanting to be with you constantly or seeking comfort in your arms. Their *desire for love and connection*, and *to feel worthy of love*, is a natural human need. The love and nurturing they need from you has a profound influence on them as they grow. Their emotional regulation is affected by the emotional climate of the family, as reflected in the quality of the attachment relationship, styles of parenting, family expressiveness and the emotional quality of the marital relationship (Sheffield Morris 2007).

Emotional support from parents has an impact on children's ability to develop positive relationships as they grow older. Children's early relationships can also impact their formal education, socialisation, resilience, self regulation and ultimately their ability to cope with life.

Parents can find these early years most challenging, particularly in understanding children's behaviour and the various stages of development they transition through.

As a parent you may feel like you are scrambling your way through each situation as it arises, sometimes handling it well and other times feeling frustrated or lost. These experiences can affect your ability to develop positive relationships with your children – your patience will be tested when your values and desires come into conflict with theirs. During these times it can be helpful to be mindful of your responses or reactions to any misalignment of values, resistance to changes and transitions your child is experiencing.

This is where it's really helpful for you to understand how your brain's responses are influenced by external experiences, by exploring the 3i's – impulsive, instinctive and intuitive responses.

Your brain is continuously firing neurons and making connections through neural pathways – taking in information and storing it as memories. When an experience or thought occurs, two neurons connect and cause a synapsis or spark. The connection between the two neurons is then fused by a layer called myelin. Myelin is an insulating layer, or sheath that forms around nerves, including those in the brain. It is made up of protein and fatty substances. This myelin sheath allows electrical impulses to transmit quickly and efficiently along the nerve cells.

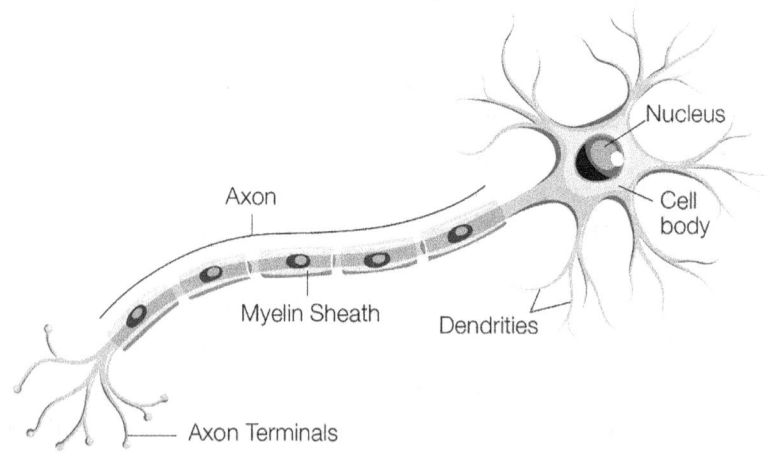

Neural network tube surrounded by myelin sheath as electrical impulses move through the neural pathway.

When children repeat actions or learn something new, they are making thousands of neural connections in their brains. They are like little sponges, soaking up information and learning from what is happening around them.

How we respond to external and internal stimuli

The following information can assist you to understand and regulate your own emotions to help you manage transitions or changes your children are going through. One main area of focus is in your responses to experiences and how the past can influence responses to what is happening in the present or how you are perceiving the future.

There are two factors involved in how we respond to experiences, interactions and changes:

1. **External factors:** things that are happening outside of your control that your brain needs to process to determine a response or reaction. Many of our decisions or reactions are based on external factors such as past experiences or other people's views, opinions or expectations, which can contribute to forming a perception in our own minds.
2. **Internal factors:** what is happening in your thought processes; how you think or feel; what is happening in your brain as you react to external factors or as you reflect on your thoughts and intuition.

Not everyone has the skills to self reflect or self regulate these emotions or factors that are taking place constantly. Your values, past experiences, and the stories that have been replayed in your mind over time play a huge role in how you respond and react to different things that are happening to you and your children.

To understand where these responses stem from and how to manage overwhelm or emotions when juggling all your responsibilities and supporting your children, let's take a closer look at the 3i's – three ways we can respond to stimuli: impulsively, instinctively and intuitively.

Impulsive (unconscious/reflexive) response

When you respond or react on impulse, you are reacting with an automatic reflex to avoid danger, pain or prey. This is often prevalent in young children, as they haven't yet learned how to think before acting. For you as a parent, it is a protective response to impending danger – you are not consciously thinking about responding, you just have an impulse to protect or avoid whatever danger is about to occur. An example might be your child running towards a road. You instantly react on impulse to protect them from danger. You may get angry or yell at them – this is a way to stop them instantly. This is your Animal Reflexive mind at work. The nerve pathways involved are the same as a reptile or amphibian responding with a reflex action to any potential danger.

Children go through different stages and rates of development when it comes to interactive and social skills. If you have ever observed a child at play, they may sometimes act on impulse – making decisions without thinking first. This is an instant reaction to whatever is happening in the environment at the time. For example, a child might reach over to grab something and bump into another child or knock something over because their impulsive brain is telling them to go and pick up the thing – they are not thinking about the consequences of the action. Your own response to this may also be impulsive, like getting angry at them for being so careless. But this is part of their learning process. Once you are more aware that this is how their brain is working at the time, your response can be more considered. When they are developmentally ready, you can teach them to be more mindful and aware of their surroundings, to think before they act, and to consider the consequences of acting on impulse. This can assist them especially as they move towards adulthood, as they need to make their own decisions and take responsibility for themselves and their actions.

Instinctive (subconscious/reflexive) response

The instinctive response is where the brain has been trained to protect you – to go into protective mode when it senses danger. If we allow our kids to take risks and get (a little bit) hurt, the brain makes a connection and knows next time to be more careful. It can subconsciously recall the past experience and next time will respond instinctively. This is why it's so important for children to learn to fall and get back up again. If you are doing the job of the brain for your child, their brain will not make the connections that give them the skills to be able to respond instinctively next time they are in that situation.

It's important to allow children's brains to make connections with your guidance along the way. It's still your role to ensure they are not in any danger, but allowing them to explore through play and rough-and-tumble games nurtures and improves their brain connections for their own protection as they become more independent.

We often use our instinctive brain when meeting new people. Our brain scans the territory, the way the person is presenting to us, how they are making us feel and whether we can trust them. The instinctive brain and intuitive brain then combine to give you a "gut feeling" about the person.

Intuitive (conscious/reflective) response

The intuitive brain is what we want to nurture for creative and critical thinking. It is the part of the brain that is activated when thinking of ideas and accessing memories. It is also the intuitive part of our minds that is not always easy to explain – children often access it when they are given time and space to create and for self-led learning. You may observe this gives them a sense of calm and balance, and brings them back to a state of enlightenment, where there is no judgement or conditioning. When children are playing or being creative, they are often in a transcendent state, or what we might call being "zoned out". This is a good thing, and allows them to listen to their intuitive brain and what it is telling them to do.

These three brain responses are important elements when it comes to understanding and managing your child's behaviour as well as recognising your own behaviours and responses to experiences you are having as your children transition through change. The easiest way to practice recognising these responses is to observe yourself through your thoughts, feelings and actions.

When a thought comes into your mind, it almost instantly becomes a feeling (impulsive or instinctive). You will have a feeling or bodily reaction to the thought (impulsive, instinctive or intuitive). Then once you have had the thought and the feeling, your body may have an instant reaction or you may choose your response intuitively. The trick is to learn how to recognise a thought, then the feeling and what actions you take by carefully considering your response.

Take some time to practice this to become more aware of how you are thinking, what you are feeling and how you are responding using one or more of the 3is. When you practice recognising these, you are able to make changes in how you respond if needed. For example, if you have a negative thought that makes you feel anxious, you are able to stop that thought in its tracks before you react. Or if your child tells you something that has happened at school and your immediate thought is to be protective of your child, you can stop that thought before you become angry or frustrated or before you take an action that may not be helpful. This is a skill that you can practice to be more mindful in your thoughts, feelings and actions or responses.

This was a gift that my coach shared with me many years ago and it changed my whole perspective and awareness of myself, who I am and how I behave. I started looking at myself and others differently. I took control of my thoughts and my emotions, became more present and could focus on why I was thinking or responding a certain way. This was the beginning of understanding myself and others at a deeper, more profound level. Having the skills to self analyse and manage myself in a more positive way had a huge impact on my relationship with my children. I saw myself and them in a new light. It helped me to get through some very tough experiences and still is one of the tools I use to stay grounded and to manage myself.

How to manage yourself through each transition

Your responses to what your children say and do influences them in many ways. Eye contact and verbal interaction with children is so important in the very early years. During this period, these interactions provide children with a way to communicate and connect in a very intuitive way. They read facial expressions and can sense and respond to your emotions from a young age. This provides them with clues as to how to behave with you or in response to you. Even now, my son - who is in his early teens - often tries to make me laugh because he finds comfort and connection with me when I am light and happy. He wants to connect with me in that moment to know that I'm ok - it is one of his highest values.

Managing changes and transitions begins with awareness of the importance of staying connected not only with your children, but with yourself. Having an awareness of the changes taking place in your child's learning and their personal development, and of your role in facilitating and nurturing those changes, can help you to manage and transition with your child as they develop, rather than resisting change. If you are part of their journey, you are able to observe and know your child and yourself at a deeper level.

When my children were young, I took each of them for walks in their pram and described to them how the day looked – I described the weather, pointed out birds, trees and trucks, and generally spoke with them about their surroundings. They couldn't speak back of course, but they were learning to listen. They listened to the sounds of the words, to the expression and tone in my voice, to the way I explained things, with their eyes fixed firmly on my face. Watching my expressions and reactions provided them with so many new skills as they transitioned to talking and interacting.

Those skills included the ability to read facial expressions, how to make eye contact, understand what I was saying to then respond, listen and take action, read my mood or the energy I was projecting, understanding and learning new words and vocabulary. Little did I know at the time that these skills were essential for their ability to learn effectively at school. To be able to listen to their teachers, read the energy in the room and respond, understand the information being presented and how to take action from the instructions provided. Understanding and responding to tone of voice and body language, how to speak with the teacher and peers and how to manage their own emotions in different situations.

These early learning experiences and conversations provided them with an understanding of their world. When my children were able to read books, each of them was able to point to a bird or a tree, a car or a bus because they recognised them through our conversations. Their brains had taken a snapshot, made the connection and stored it as a memory. They were also able to recognise the difference between reality and fiction. What you expose your children to during these early years, and throughout their education, shapes their learning in so many important ways. The skills they are learning through play, creativity, sport, rituals and traditions, spending time with family and friends and in nature, are all strengthening their brains in a way that supports their learning at school. We will explore this in further detail later in the book as we look at how you can continue to support this learning at home.

As children transition to different learning environments, being aware of their surroundings is so important for their developmental life skills. Having a sense of space and the ability to identify a safe situation and a dangerous one is an important skill to teach young children. Having conversations with them about their surroundings increases their awareness to be cautious or careful but not afraid. Explaining things in a calm and thoughtful manner is much more beneficial for their growth than having to impulsively react by yelling at them for doing the wrong thing.

It's important to always be mindful that children are still learning and they don't always learn things immediately; they need you to guide them and acknowledge when they get it right. Sometimes they need to repeat an action to learn the lesson or to recognise the consequences. This is the brain learning in action, where repetitive actions are myelinated or insulated in the brain to store the memory for later use. Of course, they will test boundaries and rules, and that, too, is a part of learning. These lessons allow you to explore how to explain more effectively how they can make more positive choices.

Your awareness of and ability to observe the connections your children make comes from spending time with them. Playing interactive games such as matching picture cards, jigsaw puzzles and other games can help them to think and see patterns and connections. As they get older, it's good to encourage them to continue to play strategy games that help them solve problems – chess, quiz games and strategy games will test their thinking. Playing games, including the online versions, can encourage their competitive nature, helping them to strive to do well.

When young children become more aware of their environment and what their peers are doing, they will no doubt be drawn to technology and the instant gratification and entertainment that devices provide. They may seek less attention from you and more of what technology has to offer.

How do you manage this change, when the value of connection can become less important to them, and the temptation of devices takes over? Through my own experience and observations as a parent over the past twenty years, I have seen my own children shift from being more interactive in the family to being more interested in social media and online games. As a result, it has been challenging to maintain a connection with each other. However, through conscious facilitation we have continued our family rituals and traditions to enable these connections. I decided once they became teenagers to have a movie and games night each Friday, to encourage my kids in these interactions. Now they are adults, we try to set aside a night each week to catch up for dinner and they can have games and movie nights with their friends to enjoy each other's company and continue to learn how to develop relationships and connections with each other.

There are various transitions you as a parent must learn to navigate as your children discover new ways to interact with their friends and family. I've also observed changes in the ways adults connect, seeking out their tribe through other pathways and portals such as online groups and forums. Whilst there is no doubt there are benefits to technology, I sometimes sense that person-to-person physical contact and interaction is changing and, possibly for some, less valued. One thing I learned during the pandemic was that connection is so important and that being with others, interacting, collaborating, having conversations and really spending quality time together is important for wellbeing and growth. This can be a priority in your family and you can contribute to making it happen.

As technology continues to evolve there are multiple ways to stay connected and to encourage interactions between you and your children. Perhaps you could brainstorm some ideas with friends and with your children to decide how you can all remain connected but still have time on social media and playing online games to strike a balance.

As your children grow and develop their interests, it's important to take notice of what they are exploring, what their passions are and what excites them. Encouraging conversation around your child's interests provides them with a sense that what they like or enjoy matters to you as well – this fulfills their value of significance, reinforcing that they matter. They then have certainty that someone in their world cares about their passions and interests.

It is important that you value their enthusiasm for certain things, even if it may not interest you or seem particularly important to you at the time. Children seek your approval naturally and if you seem disinterested, they too will soon lose interest and enthusiasm or use other unproductive ways to gain your attention.

Nurturing children's interests provides them with the freedom to explore potential future passions and professions. Children will go through many phases of things they enjoy and show an interest in, then suddenly they may change. First it might be particular toys and books they like. As they grow older they might become interested in aeroplanes or fashion. The opportunities you provide for them to explore their interests are important in forming their passions and enthusiasm for learning about new things that inspire them. Enhancing their knowledge and experiences related to their interests can lead to possible career paths, but this doesn't have to be the end goal. It's about you showing you care and sharing in what gives them joy and happiness. It validates for them that they are on the right path and is a way to encourage them to pursue those interests.

Children often don't realise they are learning or that what they learn about has a profound influence on their education and on their future work, relationship and life choices. When they are interested and engaged in something, it can be described as effortless, incidental or natural learning. When you are connected and in tune with your children, you notice their interests and can then inspire and nurture them further through each of their learning phases.

Both my daughters showed an interest in dancing at an early age. As a result of their passion for dancing, we delayed buying a coffee table so they had space to move and explore their love for dance. Constant cartwheels and choreography filled our lounge room most days and it was wonderful to see them enjoying themselves and being creative. When they were old enough, we enrolled them in a dance school to explore the passion further, as many parents do. This then led to them establishing friendships and exploring their strengths – not only their physical strength, but their strength of character as well.

After a few years, one of my daughters decided she'd had enough of dancing. At the time, I reacted quite poorly as I felt I had made many sacrifices – financial and emotional – to encourage this passion of hers. Now she was choosing to change her path. Her values had changed and she no longer wanted the *attention* that came with being on stage and having people look at her. She was a very good dancer, but she disliked the fuss made over her.

When I stopped and reflected on my reaction, I realised that I needed to tune in to what it was that she wasn't enjoying anymore. It wasn't about me. I needed to understand from her perspective that she was ready to explore something new. She was around eight years of age and going through a period of change where she was becoming more aware of herself and her place in the world. I have seen many girls begin to feel self conscious at this age, and some begin to compare themselves to others and how they fit in. This desire to fit in and feel a sense of belonging stems from the value of *significance*. My child's personality and interests were not in the world of dance anymore, and I needed to respect that and support her to explore her next interest.

She then went on to explore soccer (or football). I knew nothing about soccer so I had to be open to this new experience also. I found it confusing at first but she had a natural talent and I really enjoyed watching her as she became more confident and excelled in her new chosen sport. Even though it wasn't a sport or value I shared with her, I was willing to put aside my own attitude towards this change and learn alongside her, as well as observe the changes in her as she grew into the sport. Through this transition she was seeking significance in her own way – not by having attention while on stage, but in a team environment where she could thrive in her own strengths alongside the team. She also learned the valuable lesson of when to move on, when to persevere, what commitment means and the outcomes that can be achieved as a result of making choices.

We both learned lessons from this experience. I learned to respect her choices; she learned to take responsibility for that choice. We had discussions around making commitments, that once you decide to join a team, you are choosing to commit to being there each week, to show up and put in the effort.

Each transitional experience is about learning, not only for your children but for you too. Every experience is an opportunity to guide your children by having conversations around their choices and what they can learn from them. In this case, the decision making process of changing and learning new skills was beneficial for my daughter in understanding what she wanted to do and why. Self reflection and understanding herself were skills she acquired from this experience. These are essential life skills that often take time to learn but are crucial in developing as a person.

My younger daughter discovered a passion for interior design and decorating after watching a show on TV about renovating. I decided to work on a project with her, to indulge her passion and encourage her to explore it further. I also wanted to create a connection with her through acknowledging her passion and inspiring her to follow it. I had an old table I was no longer using and asked if she would like to strip it back, paint it and then design a new look for the entrance hallway in our home. We'd been renovating for several years and there were still many jobs to do. Now that the children were older, I thought this could be a great opportunity to teach them some handy skills for later on, when they too might need to renovate their homes.

All three of my children wanted to join in on the project. I showed them how to use the sander to strip back the paint, including all the techniques and safety precautions. I then stepped back and let them practise these new skills. I was quite amazed with the outcome. They worked together as a team to steady the table, sand back the old paint and uncover the raw timber. They took it in turns to have a go and generally co-operated to complete the tasks. Through these new experiences, they learned so many things: a new skill in using a power tool, safety skills and working with dust masks, understanding how to sand along the grain of the wood, what raw timber looks like when taken back to its natural form, and how to pack tools away for next time. So many life skills came about through a simple, fun activity.

This experience revealed to me that my children like to learn by doing and working with their hands. They love being creative and trying new experiences. This might all sound simple and straightforward, but it does take intentional thinking and consideration to provide these learning opportunities and to seize these moments to connect with your children.

The next part of the project was to design the look and feel of the room. My daughter set about drawing a design, then I showed her how to draw it on the computer using software to present the concept. She learned this new skill very quickly and before too long she was playing the role of designer, showing me – as her client – what my room would look like. She had chosen a colour scheme, style and the products that might be included. Not bad for a ten-year-old designer! She is now studying graphic design, which goes to show how these experiences can open up real possibilities and inspiration for their future career choices.

I loved watching my children transition from being reliant on me, to growing and discovering things they enjoy, and I loved having the awareness to be able to nurture their passions and to step back when necessary to let them explore and learn. I hope others can learn to love this about being a parent, too. It is in letting go that you can see them fly, transform and become their own person. This is so rewarding, even though it can be difficult to let go. When you have established a genuine connection with your children by supporting them as individuals, the transition process becomes easier because they are always connected with you through the special bond you've created.

Children often figure things out themselves if given the chance to. Sometimes we can be quick to do things for them in case they don't quite get it right the first time. Perhaps this fulfills our own need for significance in their lives. Making mistakes is a part of learning and a skill that enables us to be more creative, willing to experiment and able to push beyond our comfort zone. It's important to allow your children to make mistakes and to know that it's ok. All the greatest inventors in the world made many mistakes; the world's scientists are constantly experimenting, failing, testing and trying again. Life is about learning, exploring what is possible, and providing opportunities for growth.

> To innovate we need chaos,
> Then we need structure to make these ideas useful.
>
> SIMON SINEK (2021)

When children are learning, you need to enable a level of chaos for them to explore, experiment, make a mess and discover their strengths and interests. If they come up with an idea to create something and want to bring it to life, then there may need to be some methodical or structural process to make it happen. The ideas need chaos and the implementation requires structure. These are great skills to teach your children.

When Elon Musk, Richard Branson and Jeff Bezos each launched rocket ships, all the fanfare made it look easy. But it took many years of mistakes (and a lot of money, planning and people!) to make it work – and it still wasn't perfect. The lesson is that they dared to dream, dared to take a risk, and dared to lean into the uncertainty and chaos that it takes to turn dreams into reality. When asked what makes him successful, Musk has a simple answer, "I don't ever give up…" (Vance 2017). He is motivated to give something a chance to work, and to keep improving it until it does. The passion and drive to succeed is in the process, the uncertainty, the adventure of the journey, rather than just the end result. This is so true when it comes to children's learning.

Guiding your children through transitions is not an easy task, but if you focus on their continuous growth and development, you will soon see a natural progression taking place. If you resist these progressions, you may feel stress or anxiety, as if you are losing your children or that they are changing too fast. Allowing them to grow and spread their wings is a gift you can give them. Encourage their growth and enable them to discover who they are while helping them navigate the winding path they are on. When you are fully aware of your own growth through their changes, the transition for you can also be magical.

Chapter 4
RELATIONSHIPS

Children don't do school, they do relationships.

SCHOOL LEADER – KIDSMATTER CONFERENCE AUSTRALIA 2014

This statement – "Children don't do school, they do relationships" – had a profound impact on me when I heard it announced by a school principal at a wellbeing conference I attended in 2014. It has echoed in my ears ever since, highlighting a basic need in all of us. The message for educators, that also motivates the work I do with schools and parents, is that relationships are at the heart of everything we do and are essential for children to thrive.

Each of us manages many different relationships in our daily lives. These may include immediate family, partner, children, siblings, parents, extended family, work colleagues and friends. However, when it comes to effectively supporting children through their learning and navigating the school environment, there are four critical relationships to focus on:

1. Parent and child
2. Child and teacher
3. Parent and teacher
4. Child and peer relationships.

In this chapter, we will focus on the child-teacher relationship and the parent-teacher relationship as critical components of the partnership between home and school.

Relationship between a child and their teacher

Perhaps the most important relationship your child will have in the school environment, along with friendships they form with peers, is with their teachers. To a child, a teacher is more than an educator who is giving them information and homework! For a child to engage with and be curious about learning, there must be a certain trust or bond that forms between them and their teachers.

The child-teacher relationship is so important for children's learning. It is just as important for parents to understand that this relationship is special and, like any relationship, may sometimes need some work and time to develop. Occasionally this relationship may hit a rough patch and there may be some obstacles or challenges to work through. Each person needs to have an understanding of the other.

The relationship with their teacher can have a positive or negative impact on a child's years at school and can influence how effectively they are able to learn. Sometimes a teacher has a profound impact on a child – later in life they may still recall teachers who had a positive influence on them.

Laureate Professor John Hattie wrote about the impact teachers have on children, saying, "it is what teachers know, do and care about which is very powerful in this learning equation." He explained that "the focus is to have a powerful effect on achievement, and this is where excellent teachers come to the fore" (2003).

In order to have a powerful impact on achievement, excellence in teaching includes sharing knowledge with students in a way that is engaging, inspiring and that speaks to various learning styles and personalities in the class. It also includes teachers intentionally and purposefully caring about each individual they teach and, by doing this, enabling that relationship and the child to flourish.

In my own experience teaching young adults at university, it wasn't only the teaching that provided me with a sense of fulfilment. The most rewarding part of teaching was knowing that my students wanted to come to class to begin with, and that they were eager to learn and explore their strengths. I soon realised they were responding to my passion for teaching and wanting to draw out the best in them – for believing in them as people and acknowledging them as unique individuals.

One of the Australian Institute for Teaching and School Leadership (AITSL) teacher standards is "Know the students and how they learn" (2023). This means getting to know students' various learning styles, strengths, areas for improvement, personalities, other interests outside school, family structure, culture and traditions. It takes a very passionate and dedicated person to be able to navigate the challenges of teaching and understanding many different personalities, learning styles and abilities in a classroom. As a teacher, I saw this as an integral part of my role in engaging with my students. It taught me as much about myself as it did about them, in understanding what is most effective in teaching and learning, and always remembering that relationships are the starting point.

As a parent guiding your child through school, you will more than likely expect that teachers have the necessary training, qualifications and intellectual capacity to provide a quality education, including knowledge and practical skills that will lead your child into the next phase of their life. However, it is also important that teachers embody emotional intelligence to understand children and their needs so they are able to engage and develop positive relationships and achieve desired learning outcomes.

Hattie states:

> I have seen teachers who are stunning and demonstrably make a difference ... They question themselves, they worry about which students are not making appropriate progress, they seek evidence of successes and gaps, and they seek help when they need it in their teaching. The future is one of hope as many of these teachers exist in our schools. They are often head-down in the school, not always picked by parents as the better teachers, but the students know and welcome being in their classes (Hattie and Anderman 2011).

It is interesting that Hattie mentions teachers who are "not always picked by parents as the better teachers, but the students know and welcome being in their classes." This is important to be aware of, to avoid making any judgements or forming perceptions of teachers based on hearsay. This judgement may come from a lack of awareness of what teachers are actually doing in the classroom and in their own time to make a difference for their students. If your child is happy with their teacher, this is a huge plus as they are more likely to want to do well and to enjoy learning from them.

How do you react when there is a fractured relationship?

Perhaps you are wondering what happens if your child is not happy with their teacher. This is not uncommon and can be challenging for parents to navigate, especially when it has an impact on their child's learning or wellbeing. Many parents seek a change of teacher after observing the impact of a relationship breakdown on their child. Advocating for your child is important in this case, but the way you go about this needs careful consideration.

First, try to understand what is causing your child to feel uncomfortable with a teacher. Using the 3i's outlined earlier (impulsive actions, instinctive reactions, intuitive responses), have an initial conversation with your child, observing and listening without responding first. Then provide thoughtful guidance around how they can manage themselves with that teacher. If they have tried your suggestions and they are still finding things challenging, you may need to arrange a conversation with your child's teacher. This may seem daunting at first, but it's important to overcome any concerns or reservations you may have about raising this with the teacher.

The best approach is to make sure you don't allow emotions to take over when discussing the issues with the teacher, and to avoid coming at the situation with an attitude of blame. Relationships are not easy and it's important to keep an open mind as to what the issues are. Advocating for your child is one of your most important roles – it should be approached calmly and rationally to come to a solution.

I'd like to share with you why I wish someone had advocated for me during some challenging times with my year 4 teacher, who was particularly cruel to children and really shouldn't have been teaching. As you learned in my introduction, as a child I struggled with some difficult personal issues within my family. I was stumbling through the fallout from my parents' divorce, I had lost my grandmother, and my best friend had left the school suddenly without explanation. When I was in primary school in the 1970s, children often weren't told what was happening around them. We were oblivious to adult issues but still dealt with the emotions that stemmed from their actions, often in silence. There were no wellbeing programs or staff members who were dedicated to supporting children through these difficult times. I was very shy and although I was doing well in most of my subjects, I struggled with maths.

My teacher wasn't very tolerant of my lack of confidence in maths and often yelled at me. I felt intimidated by her anger and frustration. It was humiliating to be singled out by her, and I battled with that shame for a long time, even into adulthood. The teacher's behaviour did nothing to improve my perception of maths or my ability to learn and understand maths. Instead, I retreated and took up guitar lessons (held during maths lessons) to avoid the humiliation! I realised more recently that this, and other childhood experiences, led to my passion for ensuring children are supported by the adults around them, who should be in the right state of mind to guide children as they are learning.

Teachers who understand human behaviour and have empathy for others can better respond to and manage the many challenges that children and young adults bring to school. A few years ago one of my children was having difficulty developing a positive relationship with her year 4 teacher. It seemed it wasn't only my child who was affected – several children struggled to connect with the teacher. This resulted in poor behaviour from the children and a lack of classroom control. The children effectively shut down, switched off and refused to listen, as they had lost respect for the teacher.

My child observed the teacher as a person who wasn't connecting with the children in the class and who wasn't managing situations fairly. This lowered her opinion of the teacher and she began to behave disrespectfully. I had never experienced this from my daughter before. She had always behaved well at school and suddenly I was being informed of disrespectful attitudes. I soon realised there had been a breakdown in the relationship between my child and the teacher. My experience as a child all came rushing back to me. Having experienced a lack of intervention from my parents during a similar time in my life, my drive to advocate was probably even stronger than usual.

Instead of reacting negatively to this situation, I decided to be more proactive in solving the issues and understanding what was at the heart of the problem. I spent time talking with the teacher to provide a broader understanding of my child and why her behaviour had changed. The teacher and I discussed their relationship and how they could build some bridges. I also had discussions with my child about how she was feeling, and how she might improve the situation and her attitude towards the teacher. Over time there were some improvements, but the teacher was still not able to connect and my child wasn't able to find a way to build trust.

That was a difficult year for her – and for me – as her school work and attitude towards learning declined. I had to explain to her that she wouldn't always connect with every teacher, co-worker, boss or other person who came into her life, but that she needed to see each experience as an opportunity to learn about others and about herself. I tried to encourage her but I knew it was challenging for her.

As your child's guide and support, your patience, understanding and tolerance will help you advocate effectively and choose the most appropriate response or course of action needed. There are at least two sides to every story, so it is important to understand each perspective and how to resolve the issues together. My daughter wasn't happy with how I approached the situation with her teacher – she felt that I had taken the teacher's side – but I knew it was important to understand both perspectives and work on ways to resolve the issues. Otherwise there would be continuous conflict, which wasn't helpful for anyone.

Each year that my children have had new teachers, there has been a process to understand the relationship and its impact on the child. A teacher who is able to have conversations and share stories with the children – to give a little of themselves so the children get to know them – is a person they are more likely to warm to.

A teacher who demonstrates a genuine compassion for their learners, as well as passion towards learning themselves, will more than likely have a positive impact on their students.

A teacher who is prepared to show their vulnerabilities will appear more human and approachable, and will encourage a connection and establish respect with their learners.

Your role is to value these qualities in teachers and to encourage your child to develop a positive attitude towards their teachers. They need to respect the relationship as an important part of their learning. They will have many teachers across their lifetime and they will have their favourites, but sometimes they may have to persevere through some challenging relationships. The skills they learn through these experiences can strengthen them as people but they will need you, as their guide, to help navigate the journey.

Relationship between parents and teachers

When it comes to your child, any relationship should be important to you as their guide and support. It is just as much your responsibility to form a positive relationship with your child's teachers as it is for teachers to engage with parents. It's a reciprocal relationship and one that needs to be nurtured to enable support for your child.

During the primary years it's important to establish a good connection with your child's teachers so you are able to share information with each other that can support your child and their learning at school. When partnering with teachers, you are able to share your unique knowledge of your child. This supports teachers to engage more effectively and to have an understanding of the child. When teachers understand what children are experiencing at home and how that may impact their concentration, focus, engagement and wellbeing at school, they are better equipped to manage the child at school with empathy and understanding.

A good friend of mine and fellow parent engagement specialist, Dr Debbie Pushor from the University of Saskatchewan in Canada, has developed what she calls the opportunity to "live as mapmakers in the lives of children. When parents and teachers work together to support children, they have the opportunity to chart a course with children guided by parent knowledge" (2015).

Pushor worked alongside graduate students who enrolled in the course titled Practicum in Parent and Family Engagement. The students turned their narratives of practice into a collaborative manuscript. The subsequent publication, *Living as Mapmakers – Charting a Course with Children Guided by Parent Knowledge* (2015), explored the concept of "funds of knowledge".

> Our funds of knowledge develop out of all of our experiences, formal and informal, and, as a result, they are specific, situated, and contextual, shaped by the family and postal code into which we are born, and the family, communities, and places within which we choose to travel or reside throughout our lives. Each individual's funds of knowledge, then, are necessarily unique.

In the same publication, Pushor poses questions about what constitutes parent knowledge and asks:

> How does a parent hold knowledge of his or her child? How might that knowledge form an internal and intimate parent's map of a child? How might that map, at any point in time, reflect a knowledge of connections to people who have a shaping influence in the child's life – a kokum (Cree for grandmother), an uncle, a big sister or brother, a nanny, a make-believe friend?

> How might it highlight markers of moments and memories of significance – a first word or first step, an act of empathy, a passion pursued, an obstacle overcome, an expression of pure joy, or one of pain? How might a parent's map of a child be one that is very different from a teacher's map of that same child? What might a parent's map illuminate that a teacher's map cannot, given the different ways that parents and teachers are positioned in the life of a child and in their roles and intentions in relation to that child?

These questions are important to reflect on and answer, as they are intimately connected to the heart and soul of every child. Pushor refers to the illumination of a teacher and of a parent – the guiding lights in a child's life, each with different roles and intentions to support the child's growth.

In an interview I conducted with Pushor, we explored the positioning of parents in relation to school environments. The interview revealed the significance of the knowledge each parent has of their child, and how this can impact both their child's learning at school and their relationship with their teacher.

How can you work as a mapmaker alongside your child's teacher to support them with their learning?

The ultimate goal of Pushor's mission, which she refers to as a 'quiet revolution', is for parents and teachers to walk alongside each other to guide and support children's learning. Since my daughter began school I have been asking myself why this is not already happening. Why are parents and teachers hesitant to walk alongside each other and bridge the gap between learning at school and learning at home?

Often the structure of schooling, the demands on teachers' time and the limited opportunities available for relationship building within the school environment prevent people from establishing a strong sense and understanding of who they are and who they need to be for the child at the centre.

In her 2017 article, "Effective parental engagement is all about relationships", Dr Janet Goodall states:

> I often ask people how long their romantic partnerships would last if all they ever did was give their significant other information – if they never stopped to listen, if they never engaged in dialogue. Estimates of longevity range from a few days to a few weeks, but I've yet to find anyone who thinks that "information sharing" could be the basis of a partnership.
>
> Because it can't. Partnerships are based on shared ideas and ideals, on communication and on moving toward a shared goal; in a marriage, that might be having children or retiring early; in a school, that shared goal is for the young person in question to do as well as she/he can in the schooling system.

Much of what prevents parents and teachers from working effectively together is based on perceptions and break-downs in communication. Perceptions may include how teachers view their role as opposed to the parent role. The position of teachers as professional educators and the role of parents as a teacher is completely different. What each person is teaching is different but very much interrelated and every learning experience impacts the child both at school and at home. Parents and teachers support learning in complementary ways, yet often they remain separated, with one never daring to interfere with the other. Teachers do their job with little or no input from parents, and parents do theirs with a very brief understanding of their child as a student. By working together, each can understand the child and their needs, to enable learning to flourish in both learning environments. This separation can cause parents to feel a disconnect when it comes to their child's learning, which can in turn lead parents to challenge teachers out of frustration. This is not conducive to a flourishing relationship or a supported student.

Some teachers may have the view that parents don't value them as educators. This perception was highlighted in research conducted by

Heffernan et al., titled "The Impact of COVID-19 on Perceptions of Australian Schooling" (2021). The findings indicate that, "while teachers felt underappreciated and overworked, with 71% of teachers responding that the profession is underappreciated, public perceptions of teaching suggested that 82% of people felt the teaching profession was respected, and 93% of the public felt the teaching profession was trusted." The pandemic certainly opened up the classroom and exposed parents to the work of teachers and the lengths to which they go for students. This was a huge breakthrough and a positive result in changing perceptions of the role of teachers. "The increased knowledge and experience of seeing teachers at work resulted in social media and mainstream media campaigns celebrating the work of teachers."

So, how can you be part of the quiet revolution to change these perceptions for teachers? How can you improve your own relationships with your child's teachers to enable you to fulfill your individual role while also sharing with the teacher what can work for the child? How can you be the catalyst for change in how you perceive and value teachers and be a role model for other parents?

How to develop a positive and purposeful relationship with your child's teacher

As Pushor (2015) asserts, "When we understand funds of knowledge as personal, practical, professional, and craft, it becomes readily apparent that both teachers and parents hold rich funds of knowledge of children, teaching, and learning." If we intentionally, as partners, bring this knowledge together to create a map for supporting learning, imagine the outcomes for children.

The key words here are being intentional and purposeful in how we develop relationships to enable support for the child to occur.

Reflecting on the knowledge I have gained from my own experiences as a student, parent and professional working directly with schools, teaching students at university and learning from experts in the field such as Pushor, Mapp, Otero and Goodall, I've developed a unique formula for developing relationships in schools. It is designed as a first step to build the capacity of teachers and parents to connect and work alongside each other to support student learning and development. You can use the six steps in my PRECEDENT formula to learn how to develop positive relationships with each of your children's teachers.

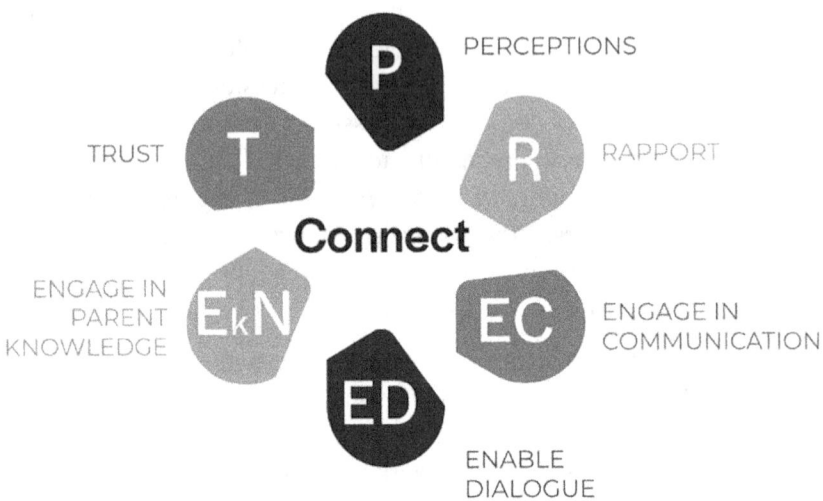

Perceptions

I am constantly fascinated by perceptions and how our brain impacts how we interact and relate to people. I'm also fascinated by the way perceptions can hold us back in so many ways – I'd like to explore this with you in the context of the relationship between parents and teachers.

Your perception of a teacher matters, but perceptions can sometimes be a hindrance when developing a connection with another person, especially when that person is someone you need to put your trust in. Your perceptions and the way you respond to and relate with the teacher have an impact not only on you and the teacher but also on the relationship your child has with their teacher.

Understanding what the challenges are that cause barriers to teachers engaging with parents and vice versa can assist us to work through ways to create positive change, and to enable engagement and genuine connection. For us to become mapmakers and work as a team, we need to be mindful of perceptions and be willing to put them aside or change them.

We depend on our senses to understand our thoughts and feelings in our outer world – everything we experience is temporary and sometimes provides information from our brains that may not be true. We then react based on that information, whether it is true or false, or whether it even exists.

Our perceptions are formed by our past experiences, family beliefs and values, and sometimes the opinions of others. Perceptions are simply ideas in our minds. They don't exist anywhere else; often they are the brain's response to a situation, experience or person.

As you learned in the last chapter, your brain is always scanning the terrain to make sure it is safe to proceed. Perceptions dictate how you respond to certain stimuli or interactions with others, both internal and external stimuli as you learned in the previous chapter. When your brain perceives someone or something to be or feel unsafe, you will respond accordingly, whether it be impulsively, instinctively or intuitively. Perceptions can therefore be deceptions – formed for various reasons that we will now explore.

When learning about coaching and how to coach, it was important for me to learn how the brain functions and how neural connections have an impact on human behaviour. My own coach and mentor, Benjamin J Harvey, explained:

> Everything we see or experience as matter, is electrical signals in the brain. The brain's interpretation of electrical signals is what we are experiencing at every moment of our lives. When photons travel through the eye, rays are turned into electrical signals that trigger neurons at the back centre of the brain – all the images and events we view are experienced through this action taking place almost unconsciously – when we see, touch, hear, taste, we are observing electrical signals being received in our brains – an electrical copy is formed in the brain and myelinated as a memory or experience that our brains can then find when a need arises (2018).

To expand on this further, each time an electrical connection is produced in the brain, a sheath of myelin wraps around that connection, much like applying a layer of tape around an electrical cord where two pieces meet in the middle. This layer of fat insulates the connection, allowing information to flow freely through what is called a neural pathway. These pathways are essential for the brain to transmit information throughout the body.

This is why when we think about something or learn something repeatedly, the brain is able to quickly access the information through that clear, insulated pathway. This is essential for learning and is connected to all the thoughts, feelings and emotions you have on a daily basis. It is also how we form perceptions through memories.

When you experience an event that is fun and exciting and you replay it in your mind, you are able to tap into that electrical copy in the brain and experience the same feelings in your body and mind. Likewise, if you have experienced something traumatic, replaying the same story over and over can cause repeat trauma, triggering a perception from that experience and what it has led you to believe. It is a story you tell yourself and the more it is repeated, the more you believe it because the information is being imprinted or embedded in your brain.

Behaviours and beliefs and how they impact relationships

When we think about any relationship it always begins with an initial connection. As humans, we usually work out subconsciously as well as consciously whether we can trust a person, if it is safe to open up with them and if we can continue to move towards a relationship of some kind.

Your own experiences at school may have been good or not so great. Childhood experiences often shape the perceptions that we take with us into adulthood. It is worth remembering that as parents you may be experiencing school for the first time since being a student yourself. Even setting foot on the school grounds can trigger memories, past experiences and sometimes even trauma or fear.

When you meet a teacher or school staff member for the first time or as you get to know them, it helps to be mindful of any perceptions that you may have. Think about how you feel when you are in their presence or having a conversation with them. Are they ensuring you feel safe and heard? Are you also giving them space to feel safe with you? Are you viewing them through a non-judgemental lens? Listen to your thoughts and feelings, think about what your body is doing, how your physiology is responding. Are you feeling calm with a regular heartbeat or are you feeling nervous or intimidated? Why are you feeling this way?

Perceptions formed by the subconscious mind are a major factor in who we are, in our personalities, in how we interact with others, the decisions we make and so on. They impact how we think, feel and act towards others and are very powerful factors when it comes to building a connection with someone. It is your awareness of your perceptions that matters most because you have the ability to shift your perception through rational and intuitive thinking, rather than through impulsively forming a perception of someone.

Rapport

Another effective way to form a connection with someone is to build rapport. Rapport building is a skill that comes naturally to some but not to everyone and it has the power to break down any misperceptions when it is applied in an intentional way. It is absolutely essential to create a connection with another person.

Rapport building is about creating a sense of commonality, of sameness and likeness so that people feel comfortable with each other and are therefore able to communicate more effectively to develop a relationship and ultimately, trust. The word rapport comes from the French word Rapporter. In 1660 the word was coined to describe an interaction between two people, "bearing, yield, produce; harmony, agreement" (Online Etymology Dictionary 2023).

In 1975 two researchers, Charles Berger and Richard Calabrese, developed a theory to assist in the development of rapport. They called the theory the Uncertainty Reduction Theory (URT) with the aim being to reduce uncertainty for the other person so that rapport flows easily. (Gilmour 2019).

This theory effectively asks each person to make sure the other person feels certain about them during the interaction. It's about helping someone feel comfortable in your presence, so they are able to open up, show vulnerability and express themselves. Creating and enabling rapport between yourself and another person means you've taken the time to be intentional in how you reduce uncertainty for them. This may include simple methods such as a welcome greeting, a smile, listening and responding in a way that shows you have heard them.

It's especially important to understand how to build rapport if it's the first time you are meeting with your child's teacher. You may feel unsure of what to say, how to approach them and how to overcome any perceptions you may have of teachers or of that particular person. Check in with yourself on how you are viewing the teacher in front of you then put aside your perception and focus on making sure the other person feels comfortable in your presence.

Perhaps the first time you meet your child's teacher will be at parent-teacher meetings. This can be very daunting for some people, especially if you have had a challenging experience as a child at school. It is worth noting that some teachers are just as nervous as you are, so building rapport using the Uncertainty Reduction Theory will help break the ice and make it easier to have meaningful conversations about your child who is their student.

Vocal rapport

Start with vocal rapport by initially finding something you have in common to talk about and helping the other person feel comfortable. The common ground you both have is the child at the centre. Focusing on your child is the best starting point and a way to find a common interest.

You may wish to start off with casual conversations about your child, perhaps by sharing what your child does outside of school in the community. Sharing what you know about your child and their interests can make conversation flow more easily. You and the teacher may know the same people or have a common interest that you can discuss. These types of conversations break down or reduce any barriers.

Verbal communication is more than just talking about subject matter, it includes tone of voice, pacing your conversation, pitch, volume, phrasing, breathing and accents. If you do have an accent, slow down your pace so that the teacher is able to understand what you are saying. Your volume should be loud enough to hear but not too loud that it becomes overbearing or dominating. Your tone of voice should match the tone of the other person and rise and fall as the conversation moves along.

Physical rapport

Physical rapport is being aware of your physiology, including how you stand, where you place your hands, how you are sitting and how you are able to make eye contact. Your posture is important as it shows your interest in the conversation. Your physiology sends many messages to the other person; if you notice something about how you are presenting to them physically, you are able to change it.

Eye contact is a very important physical aspect of building rapport. Making eye contact can show the other person you are listening and present in the conversation. Avoiding eye contact might indicate you are nervous or perhaps that you're not interested in the conversation.

> People like people who are like themselves or
> who are like how they would like to be.
>
> ANTHONY ROBBINS

Matching and mirroring

When building rapport, matching and mirroring is a technique you can use to help synchronise yourself with the other person. By subtly matching or mirroring what the other person is doing – how they are standing, how they are holding themselves, where they place their hands – you can provide a sense of understanding and comfort by mirroring these actions. This helps them feel at ease in the conversation, as long as it is not too obvious. Being subtle in your approach is more effective than forcing yourself to mirror them.

Keyword mirroring

This is about active listening and responding to show you understand. In other words, you are listening to respond intuitively based on what they have said to you, not impulsively or instinctively. You are engaged in the conversation and are able to respond in a thoughtful way with consideration of the words you use, how you repeat or rephrase what they have said and how you frame an answer or ask a question.

Sensory systems

These are visual, kinesthetic and auditory senses that are active throughout all interactions. They are connected to emotion. Some people are more visual and will focus on body language and what it is communicating to them. Others are more kinesthetic and may like to touch or make a gesture, by placing a hand on your arm or shaking hands. Other people are more auditory and will be listening intently to your tone of voice, your words and taking in the messages you are sending them. All of these types of interactions send signals to the brain for you to know how to respond.

Energetic connection

Energies are unseen but can be felt by most people participating in any interaction. Some people are more in tune with energies than others – children with autism, for example, can experience high sensitivity and an acute awareness of internal body cues and sensations (known as interoception) (Autism Speaks 2023).

You can usually tell how the energies are impacting you by how you feel when you meet someone. If they are friendly and welcoming, or if they are cold, you can usually tell. Or you may feel unsafe around them. According to Association for Psychological Science President Lisa Feldman Barrett, this is "more than just a feeling, it's an internal response to the energy of the other person. Interoception is your brain's representation of sensations from your own body – it is the sensory consequence of this activity, and is central to everything from thought, to emotion, to decision making, and our sense of self" (Armstrong 2019).

Building rapport is a skill that will help you to break the ice between yourself and teachers. There are many teachers who feel trepidation around parents and who may need to be reassured that you are not a threat in any way. Demonstrating positive interactions through building rapport can assist in nurturing a relationship that enables you to work together to support your child.

Engage in communication

Schools will constantly provide information for you to be informed of activities happening at the school and what is required for your child to be organised for sport or excursions etc. Initially you may feel bombarded by all the different types of communication coming at you, however there are reasons for the communication and it's important to read and engage in what is being sent to you.

Much of the communication may be information only and may not require a response, but at times you will need to take action. If you are new to the school routine, it is important to be on top of dates and upcoming events so that you can plan to attend if possible. When your child is in the early years of school. you will need to help them be organised for sport days or other events, to remind them to have their clothes ready or their dress up outfit, books or other materials ready for the next day. As they get older, you may just mention in conversation the need to be organised, to jog their memory and to show them you are supportive and interested.

Communication from school about learning provides opportunities for teachable moments at home. You can leverage what you know about your child's learning and enhance their learning-at-home experiences.

For example, if your child is learning about the planets or the environment, you may take them to the library to explore books on specific topics they are learning about at school. The more communication about learning the better, as it enables you to support learning at home in simple ways. Engaging with the communication from your child's teacher may include developing a new understanding of terminology and the language used in learning. This may have changed since you were at school so it's important to either ask your child to explain or talk with the teacher to discuss any language or terminology you're unsure about.

If there is little or no communication coming home from school, you are allowed to ask for more information and opportunities to understand what your child is learning and how you can support them at home. Always ask questions if you are unsure and if you need further support to understand how your child is progressing through their learning.

> Listening is not simply hearing the words that are spoken
> Listening is understanding why the words were spoken.
>
> SIMON SINEK

Enable dialogue

Enabling dialogue means you are available to talk with the teacher about your child and their learning in a two-way conversation. This should include listening as much as talking. Throughout my children's education I was able to meet with their teachers twice a year or make another time to see them to discuss my children. I had varied experiences at these meetings with different teachers. Some were very open to conversation but others delivered one way information that didn't really provide any opportunity for dialogue. Two-way conversations are important as they demonstrate a willingness to work together to find a solution or share information that is relevant and that supports your child. As we explored earlier, once you build rapport with your child's teacher, conversations can flow more easily. Even if you have to engage in a challenging conversation, you will have established a connection that may make it easier to discuss your child.

When your child first begins school you may find it challenging to find an appropriate time to talk one-on-one with their teacher. Most schools will have processes to enable you to communicate with teachers either via apps, email or making a specific time to meet with them. Always consider that teachers have multiple students each day to keep track of, to settle at the start of the day and to prepare for leaving at the end of the day, so they are not usually available during these times.

Whenever you are seeking dialogue with a teacher, whether it be to share something about your child, to raise a concern or to ask a question, it's important to remember that teachers may not have all the answers. It is important to work together to find solutions for the child at the centre. Teachers are not social workers and they can't be expected to solve social or family issues but, if they are aware of your circumstances, they can be mindful and empathetic towards your child. The school may be able to recommend further support for you and your family if needed.

During parent-teacher conferences, having a two-way conversation is more productive than just the teacher talking to you. It's good practice to have a few questions ready and information to share about your child so you don't miss this opportunity for dialogue. Always ask, "How can I support my child's learning at home?" so that you are able to integrate enhanced learning opportunities into your family context. You can also share with the teacher what you are already doing at home, to see if it aligns with what your child is learning. Having a discussion about how you can support at home could open up many opportunities for you and the teacher to work together.

If there is a conversation about your child and what they may be struggling with, work with the teacher on how you can explore ways to help your child achieve their learning goals. If you are not aware what their learning goals are, ask their teacher to explain them and how you can provide support that will help them feel more confident, whether it be socially or academically. Open conversations between the adults who surround children are critical for supporting each child to thrive in their learning.

Engage in parent knowledge

In the partnership between yourself and your child's teacher or teachers, your knowledge of your child can provide the teacher with extra information to support their student. As you learned earlier from the work of Dr Debbie Pushor, you hold funds of knowledge about your child that teachers don't have. You are in a unique position to observe your child at home: how they learn, what their likes, dislikes, challenges, passions and interests are. You know what makes them laugh, what makes them sad and what habits they have that may have an impact on their learning at school. From this, you can share relevant information with the teacher.

Everything about being a human impacts how we learn and behave in different environments. As parents you may observe how your child is in the home and be quite surprised when a teacher shares how different they are at school. Often this is because they are adapting to different personalities, rules, boundaries and environments so they may feel they need to adjust their personality, behaviours and traits to feel they belong or to be accepted.

Other things to share about your child include their interests and passions, what books they enjoy reading, how they learn and how they are adapting to school, what sort of emotions and experiences they share with you about school, or any challenges they are having at home that could affect their learning or socialising at school. Always be mindful of your child's privacy, as well as how sharing information may impact the relationship between teacher and student. The sharing of parent knowledge is probably not something that you would do until you trust the teacher and have an understanding of what they will do with the information you choose to share. This can take some time – you need to get to know the teacher to know that the information you are sharing is not going to be used inappropriately or against your child or your family. This is possibly why many parents withhold information from schools; they either feel ashamed to share certain information or they haven't yet built trust with the teacher to feel confident in sharing. Often schools don't provide many opportunities for parents and teachers to develop trusting relationships as there are limited times for interactions and getting to know each other. This then means there are missed opportunities for information sharing between parents and teachers. You can initiate this to ensure your child's teachers know your child and how to inspire them in their learning.

Knowledge of children and how they learn is related to professional practice in education and therefore teachers should be seeking to know the children they teach on more than just a surface level. I recall sharing information about my son with a teacher which made a huge difference to his learning in year 3. His teacher shared with me that he was easily distracted in class and she was constantly having to tell him to stop being disruptive. I shared with the teacher that there are certain children he was distracted by and that he was also a very quick learner and was highly motivated to learn when he could see the purpose of what he was learning. She then explained that they were implementing a new teaching strategy called visible learning and that she could show him how he was progressing and where he needed to improve or get to next. We both discussed this as a strategy that could be more motivating for him once he could see a purpose or reason for what he was learning. We hoped therefore that he would be more interested in completing tasks to get to the next level rather than allowing himself to get too distracted.

He was and still is a fast learner – once he grasped a concept, he was ready to move onto the next thing. So the teacher and I came to an agreement and we monitored my son's progress over the next term. By the end of the term, he had improved, was less disruptive in class and was able to be more engaged in his learning.

This was an example of me sharing my funds of parent knowledge and advocating for my child, who could have potentially been disruptive for the whole year had I not had that discussion with the teacher. The teacher had also shared her funds of knowledge about him in the classroom which was important for me to know. How I responded to this information was to focus on my child and how to shift his behaviour by focusing on his strengths rather than what he was doing wrong. It demonstrated how we could come to a solution together to benefit both the teacher, who was trying to manage a class full of children at all different levels, and the student.

Sharing parent knowledge is an essential part of your role when you are advocating for your child. Their strengths and their challenges do impact their learning, and I encourage you to share what you can to support their teachers to understand them, and to show that you are available to work through solutions with the teacher should your child need extra support.

In such a mutually supportive relationship between parent and teacher, there should be few issues, especially when the child is at the centre of the discussion and there is cooperation and collaboration between the people involved.

Trust

Trust is possibly the most important thing for you to develop with your child's teacher – we touched on this earlier when exploring perceptions. Your perceptions of a teacher can impact the trust you develop with them.

When you enroll your child in a school, it is usually based on the promise of trust. That the school can be trusted to educate your child, your most valuable possession. That your child will be safe, nurtured, supported, guided in their learning, and that they will come out the other end with the promise of a future.

Trust is a sense that you get when you meet someone. As your brain forms perceptions it is a feeling we get when we feel safe, secure, acknowledged, supported, valued, validated, seen, and heard.

Trust is a feeling you get when you feel comfortable, safe and confident that you are being heard, accepted, welcomed and valued by another person.

Trust is a feeling we get when our values are met and our beliefs are validated and believed by others.

Think about well known brands that you trust. What is it that they do that helps you to trust them?

But what breaks that trust? A faulty product, a lack of support? Poor systems to manage any support problems or other issues that arise? What are the feelings you get when things go wrong? Anger, frustration, disappointment. There is a reaction or a response you have when trust is broken. A lack of trust can bring up these emotions in people, which is why it's critical to continue to nurture trust.

You may not gel with every single teacher who teaches your child but your main focus should be on how well they are able to understand and teach your child, as well as how they communicate with you. If you have any reservations about the teacher, you may need to either work on that and put aside any negative feelings or perceptions you may have, or you may wish to raise it with their direct leader or school principal.

Trust in yourself. When you are able to trust your intuition, you can then make more considered decisions when it comes to parenting, how you present yourself, how you lead by example, how you respond and advocate for your child and how you develop a positive relationship with your children's teachers over the many years you are involved in the school system. I encourage you to be intentional in establishing trust by using the steps I've suggested for all relationships and gaining knowledge of how to improve in each area.

Chapter 5

ROLES AND RESPONSIBILITIES

> Let's make it known that a parent is not solely someone
> who is biologically a parent but, rather, it is anyone who parents.
> A parent is an auntie or uncle, a grandma or grandpa,
> a kohkum or moshom, a nanny or caregiver, the partner of
> a parent, a stepparent … or ANYONE who "parents" a child.
>
> DR DEBBIE PUSHOR (2023)

When I first began the journey through school with my eldest daughter, I was fairly confident that I had prepared her well for what lay ahead. Little did I know at the time that my roles and responsibilities as a parent would change dramatically. I would need to adjust and be flexible throughout the journey with my eldest and each of my children after her.

In this chapter I will explore the role of parent, which ties in with parent identity. Use of the word parent when it comes to "parent engagement" means those who are the main carers of children, whether they are biological parents or not. I have had many discussions about this with people who feel the word is too restrictive and leaves out the important role family members and others in the community also have in children's lives. However, the role of parent is unique and distinct from that of the role of family.

Pushor often talks about this in her work, sharing that:

> In speaking about language and the conceptualizations behind why we use the language we do, let's define the word "parent" as we use it. While much of the field has moved away from the term "parent engagement" and to the term "family engagement," we continue to talk about parents, as well as families, and here's why. We never talk about schools without talking about teachers. We never talk about schools without talking about principals ... or educational assistants ... or custodians. Why? Because each role is distinct and important. The same is true in a family. There are roles that are distinct and important – and thus worthy of naming. To parent, a verb, means to play a primarily caregiving role in a family, assuming responsibilities for such things as income, housing, and food security; assuming responsibilities for holistic nurturing and direction; assuming responsibilities for family decision-making and leadership. So, rather than rejecting the word parent for fear that it is too reductive or exclusive, let's reclaim the word and redefine it according to the parameters of who fulfills the role of a parent and what it means to be a parent (2013).

Your role as parent

Your role in supporting your child through their education and learning journey may not be explained to you by the school unless they are extremely well versed and invested in supporting parent engagement. There may be an expectation that you should know what your role is, but as a parent experiencing school with your child for the first time, it's not always obvious.

First and foremost, your role is to be your child's parent. By this I mean that you assume the role of parent as explained in Pushor's definition – the first person to influence your child, instilling the values and providing the guidance and support you believe will benefit them as they move through life. Parents' focus needs to be on what is happening with children at home, but also needs to keep pace with what is happening at school, considering how to interact with and integrate their learning into the family and home life, thus enhancing their opportunities at school and beyond.

Through my work in exploring and advocating for parent engagement as an essential component of a child's learning success, I draw on the

Dual capacity-building framework for family-school partnerships (2019) developed by Mapp and Bergman for the US Department of Education.

The Dual Capacity Framework is widely used as a guide for schools in how to design strategic plans and opportunity conditions to enable family-school partnerships. It maps out guidelines for schools to achieve equity in education through capacity building of teachers and parents, enabling engagement in student learning to improve outcomes and opportunities for all children.

The Framework outlines the essential conditions – Process Conditions and Organisational Conditions – that need to be in place in the school learning environment to enable effective engagement in learning:

Process conditions
1. Linked to learning
2. Relational
3. Asset based
4. Culturally responsive and respectful
5. Collaborative and interactive.

Organisational conditions
1. Systemic – embraced by leadership across the organisation
2. Integrated – embedded in all strategies
3. Sustained with resources and infrastructure.

From a school perspective, the roles of the school to enable and facilitate engagement in learning are outlined in the framework. From a parent perspective, these can also be adapted in the home, along with an understanding of your various roles and responsibilities as the supporter of your child's learning and overall development.

Aim for the 4c's
1. **Confidence** – developing your confidence as a parent who is able to support your child at home with their learning.
2. **Connection** – with your child's learning and school community.

3. **Cognition** – understanding your child's learning strengths, gaps, goals and how to support these alongside teachers and your child.
4. **Capacity** – to engage in their learning so they can reach their full potential.

In my coaching practice I draw on this framework as part of professional and personal development for teachers and parents to develop each of these capacities that enable effective parent engagement.

In understanding how to develop these capacities, it's important to look at the different roles and responsibilities you have to enable engagement in learning. The roles are many and varied and can be defined as the following.

The Dual Capacity Framework outlines the parent roles and responsibilities as:
- Supporters
- Encouragers
- Monitors
- Advocates
- Decision makers
- Collaborators.

The Global Family Research Project (Weiss et al. 2018) describes the roles of parents as:
- Volunteers and leaders
- Networkers and community builders
- Co-learners
- Advisor, monitor, mentor and coach
- Negotiator and connector
- Path builder and co-creator
- Data analyst
- Decision maker
- Advocate and change agent.

Through my work with schools developing teams of parents and teachers to work together, we unpack the roles and responsibilities of parents. To help you understand the "how" of your role as parent when supporting your child through school, I have combined the ideas from parents and teachers, with the definitions of the parent roles from the Dual Capacity Framework and Global Family Research Project. I have then explored practical examples of how you can effectively carry out these roles, integrated within your family context and your own parenting style.

Parents as volunteers and leaders

Over my time as a student and working with schools, the role of parents in schools has mostly been to be "involved". This essentially means doing things for the school and immersing yourself in the school community as a volunteer. Being involved and doing things for the school is involving yourself and your family in community and utilising some of your talents and skills to benefit the school and students.

Parent involvement programs "tend to be directed by the school and attempt to involve parents in school activities." Typically, parents are asked to serve in roles as "audience, spectators, fundraisers, aides and organizers" (McGilp & Michael, 1994). Benson (1999) notes that the word involvement "comes from the Latin, *'involvere,'* which means 'to roll into' and by extension implies wrapping up or enveloping parents somehow into the system" (p. 48). Beare adds that "the implication in the word is that the person 'involved' is co-opted, brought into the act by another party" (Benson, 1999, p. 48).

Being involved is often about following the school's agenda, but also about giving before receiving and not necessarily expecting anything in return, not even recognition for your efforts, "while knowledge, voice and decision-making continue to rest with the educators" (Pushor, 2001).

As an involved parent, you are unselfish in your attitude and willing to commit to making a difference for the whole school community, even if it is only in a small way. Your presence at the school demonstrates to your child that you care about their learning community and the other world they enter each weekday. Your positive and active involvement contributes to their positive attitude towards school and gives them the confidence that you are a part of the community as a family.

Being involved provides opportunities for schools to develop relationships with parents and other family members. Parents who are physically present in the school are able to get to know and form relationships with the staff. This then enables you to develop a strong partnership with your child's teacher to enhance your child's learning experiences. You have the opportunity to have adult-to-adult conversations with the teacher when required. It has become more challenging for parents to be involved in schools with both parents working and other demands on their time. It has therefore become a challenge for schools to organise events where parents attend to volunteer. This has meant a shift in priorities for schools to organise events that provide parents with the tools for supporting learning at home rather than the expectation of parents to volunteer.

An involved parent:

- Dedicates time to attend working bees, join fundraising activities, work in the canteen or volunteer to help teachers either in or out of the classroom.
- Takes their child to and from school each day and ensures they are there on time with the correct uniform and other essential items they need.
- Reads newsletters, responds to notes and emails, signs permission forms and makes sure children are prepared for excursions and sport days.
- Joins a committee or forms a committee for a specific purpose in making a difference for the school community.
- Becomes a member of the school board or advisory committee to be involved in endorsing decisions for the benefit of the whole school community.

Supporting activities as a volunteer involved in the school provides positive role modelling for children in the development of community and helping others. It also demonstrates to your child that you respect their learning community and being a part of their journey.

Being involved not only benefits children, it also helps you as a person to grow and build relationships with others. This then reflects on the children, who learn by the example their parents provide when developing relationships with other adults – modelling positive relationships is essential learning for children.

Your involvement benefits the school by:

- Developing an enhanced learning environment for the children both inside and outside the classroom.
- Lending support for children and others in the community.

- Empowering parents as leaders in the school, providing positive role modelling for other parents and all children.
- Contributing to a feeling of belonging to a caring and welcoming community, where everyone helps each other – a village raising the children.

I can honestly share that volunteering in my children's school was a very rewarding experience for me. Not only was I able to lead by example for my children, I was also acknowledged by students who knew me by name and knew I was a leader in the community. I was able to get to know the students and their families, and other parents sought me out for advice and support. The school principal recognised my leadership, even though at the time I didn't see that in myself. He offered me the opportunity to lead a parent group in the school. This was the catalyst that led me to the work I am doing today, supporting parents and teachers to work together in partnership for children.

You never know where being a volunteer leader in your school might lead you. For me, it began a whole new journey in my career. I have now led many other parents and school communities on this journey, impacting students and their development in ways I could never have imagined.

While volunteering is a noble and impressive thing to do for yourself, your child and the school community, there are other roles that you have that impact your child and their learning and development. Perhaps you are seeking more connection with your child beyond the scope of volunteering. This is where your role at home is so valuable.

Parents as facilitators of learning at home

When you are considering your child's learning journey, it is important to think about how you are setting the scene or creating "process and opportunity conditions" for facilitating learning at home. Here are some simple ideas to consider in how you can set the scene for your child to be on a continuous learning process, inside and outside of the classroom:

Creating opportunities for incidental learning

By incidental learning, I mean learning opportunities that happen out of the blue or are not planned or controlled. They may be simple things you do each day, which might include learning that aligns with what your children are learning at school – for example, you can share with your children examples of maths and science in cooking, sport, etc.

If your child is learning about numbers, you might play a game to see how many numbers they notice while you are out and about. One of my children was playing with our neighbour's child one day at my home and they were talking about odd and even numbers that they were learning about at school. I took this opportunity to support their learning by suggesting they walk up the street together to find the odd and even numbers on the letterboxes. This gave them the enhanced learning to become familiar with the shapes of the numbers and to say the numbers out loud. They also learned that odd numbers are on one side of the street and even numbers are on the other. These incidental learning moments are available when you are aware and listening to what your children are sharing with you. If you create opportunities for enhancing their learning, it broadens their awareness that learning is everywhere, that what they learn at school connects with the world around them and that learning is fun.

Setting the scene for their learning environment at home

Provide a quiet space in your child's bedroom or in your kitchen or living room where you can interact with them and have conversations about their learning while they do homework or create.

You can motivate them to do homework or learn at home by asking them to create their own learning environment or space where they feel comfortable. They might decorate it or set it up in a way that suits them so they feel a sense of ownership of that space. There are many items you can purchase to help them learn to organise their things. They might colour co-ordinate, or set up a desk space that has character and shows off part of their personality. They may like to listen to music while they create or do their homework. Giving them the space to design how they want to learn is a step towards more enjoyment of learning.

Provide opportunities for creative thinking and making by purchasing things like stencils, colouring books, or sketch pads for drawing or painting or asking your family to give these as gifts for your children for birthdays or other gift giving celebrations.

You may also take your child to a remnants or craft shop to purchase various mediums for them to explore and create at home. If you can't afford to purchase materials, you could ask a family member or friend if they might have some materials your child could use or enquire at the school or local council for any other ways to access art and craft materials for your child.

Have books easily accessible and on display so your child knows that reading is valued and a part of your family culture and routines. Ask them to choose a book for you to read together so they learn to make decisions and take ownership of their choices and learn at home. This also teaches them to share their learning with you.

Creating a culture of learning at home that is fun, easy to do, that doesn't take up too much time but instead is integrated with your family life will benefit your child's learning both at home and at school.

Opportunities for enhanced learning

When facilitating family activities, consider how they are contributing to all types of learning for your child. Opportunities for enhancing learning are everywhere. Whether you are at home or out in the community visiting family and friends, going on holidays or going to different events or locations, there are many opportunities for children to learn. Benefits of being outdoors and providing other experiences include:

- Exercising
- Learning about and connecting with nature
- Discovering animals and the wonders of the environment around them
- Navigating different terrain through walking, running, climbing to enhance coordination and spatial awareness
- Different sensory experiences through smelling the air and trees, touching and feeling textures and sensations
- Feeling a sense of freedom
- Developing an awareness of surroundings
- Learning about people and other cultures
- Broadening awareness of nature through observation
- Sensory, visible, auditory and kinesthetic experiences – seeing, hearing, touching, smelling and tasting and many more.

As you expose children to different environments, talk with them about their experiences. Discuss what they see, how they feel, and what they imagine. This is a great way to enhance their learning about their surroundings, the environment and life outside of their normal routine. These experiences can support their imagination and shape ideas that can enhance their writing and creative skills. When they have experiences and create memories, they are able to share their stories and make connections between nature, other surroundings and learning environments.

Playing board games, cooking, bushwalking, exploring, playing sport, visiting relatives, and eating out at restaurants are just some examples of learning environments and opportunities you can utilise to help your child see what is happening around them while also linking that learning with what they learn at school. Of course, children do need downtime and learning doesn't have to be constantly facilitated or pointed out. Allowing them time on their own to just relax and play is just as important. Choose teachable moments when the opportunity arises but if it is too often, children may tune out. Be aware when these opportunities arise and consider how to make the most of them when appropriate.

Think about what skills your children are learning through activities and experiences. One example is playing board games and online games – these teach children how to follow rules and stick to them; how to play fairly with others; how to persevere and reach the next level; how to negotiate and cooperate; how to lose; how to win; how to strategise and think about how to complete a task or win the game. Another example is cooking – this can teach children how to follow directions or instructions; how to prepare in advance; how to measure and use maths ; how to be patient; how to use equipment safely in the kitchen; how to clean up after themselves and how to provide for others.

These activities are examples of everyday occurrences that present simple yet essential learning opportunities. When you recognise the value of each experience you provide or enable for your child, you will realise how important your role is in supporting their learning and development at home.

As a facilitator of learning at home, you are effectively creating process conditions and opportunities for learning the various skills children need to know to be able to manage at school and in life.

Perhaps the greatest gifts that learning and a formal education can give to a child is the ability to think, to be creative and to solve problems, and you have the capacity to facilitate this for your children in ways that suit your family context and your capacity at home.

Parents as networkers and community builders

When you become a member of a school community, it opens up opportunities to develop new relationships. A school is not just a place for educating children, there are many new people to meet and connect with. As a parent you are able to network with other parents and be a part of developing the community culture you would like your children to learn in.

Your role as networker and community builder is to learn about others, get to know them and work together to build community. When you network with others you're able to make connections that can enhance the school community but that also may lead to other benefits. Getting to know your children's friends' parents for example is important so you are able to make arrangements for the children to connect outside of school, but also to be able to manage any issues that may arise in their friendships.

Networking can not only help you to broaden your social network but also your business network, should you run your own business or have a specific skill set that could be useful for others. Some schools tap into the strengths of parents and their skills to teach other parents and the students – you are a valuable asset within a school community when you bring people together to feel welcomed and valued. I have witnessed this in action in many school communities and the energy it brings to the school environment is amazing. It impacts how children feel when all the adults who surround them create an environment of safety, fun and a thriving school culture that embraces a diverse group of people from all walks of life.

When you are a significant part of creating a relational culture within your school, many parents will share this with others in their community. This then strengthens the appeal of the school but also impacts how children are influenced by the adults in the community. Many of the parents I've come across who are involved in their school, genuinely have a passion and interest in strengthening their communities so other children and families can benefit from having a wonderful place to learn and grow. You are able to leave a legacy that is genuinely purpose driven to have an impact on children, so seizing these opportunities can provide you with positive experiences in the school environment.

Parents as co-learners and collaborators

There are many opportunities for schools to engage parents as co-learners and collaborators. I was lucky enough to be recognised by a school leader who saw the value in the many skills and strengths of parents, and who was willing to collaborate and work with them to improve the school for the children and their families.

One of the ways we engaged parents as collaborators was to ask them to share their skills with children. One of the parents in the community was an electrician so he was invited in to share his knowledge with the students when they were learning about electricity. Another parent with a young baby was invited to come in with the baby to share knowledge of the growth of a child with the students as they were learning about this in class. These types of opportunities are a great way to demonstrate learning in context and to show children how their learning at school is connected with life.

Learning is a continuous process. When children learn from different influences and are enabled to make those important neural connections, their minds are broadened and their interest in learning is strengthened as they are more curious about learning.

Parents as co-learners alongside children sets a positive example for children to know that learning continues as you move into adulthood – and that they can teach their parents a thing or two. When they are able to express their learning, it reinforces their understanding of knowledge and allows them to retain that information and see that you value what they are learning.

When children are encouraged to share with you, it's important you listen and take an interest to validate for them your availability to support their learning.

Parents as advocates

No-one knows your child better than you do. You are their first and most important role model. Therefore, you are more than likely the first person to know and notice that something isn't quite right or that you need to speak up for your child and give them your attention and support.

Sometimes this can be a little daunting, especially if you are not sure how to go about raising a concern or if you haven't met or built rapport with their teacher yet. It's important to know that if you don't ask questions, there may be no improvement for your child – whatever the issue is, it may become bigger if not addressed.

You are absolutely the best person to advocate for your child. So how do you advocate in a way that is going to make a difference and have a positive impact for your child?

Here are some of the ways you can approach teachers in a positive way so that you are able to work together to support your child.

1. Build a healthy respect and rapport with the teacher and help them understand any concerns you might have for your child, whether it be related to their wellbeing or their academic learning.

2. Plan ahead before responding to a situation that has come to your attention. Carefully consider using your intuitive responses, reflecting on the situation first. Decide what you would like resolved or what support you feel your child needs to improve in their learning or wellbeing. Think about whether it's something you can support your child with at home (as a family or one to one), if it is a team effort alongside the teacher or if it is something for the school leaders to resolve.

3. Write down what you would like to say first so you are careful in how you approach a subject, using words that are not attacking but calm, purposeful and thoughtful.

4. Keep records. For example, if your child shares information with you, write this down so you have a record of any incidental details they have shared with you. You will then have evidence of the specifics rather than accidentally exaggerating or down-playing a story. If you feel it is appropriate, you may wish to invite your child along to the meeting to share their story or version of events – but give them the choice rather than putting them in a position they don't feel comfortable to be in. Should you bring your child to the meeting, be mindful of how you are interacting with the teacher and what you are demonstrating to your child in how to manage challenges in a calm and considered way. Listen and respond with respect even if you disagree with the teacher's perspective.

5. Ensure you are not approaching the situation from a place of blame – it's always better to have your emotions under control so you can

think rationally before approaching the teacher with a question. Teachers have more than just one child in the classroom to be aware of, so it's possible they may not have noticed something that you have noticed or that your child has brought to your attention. Give the teacher the benefit of the doubt until you've had a conversation about the matter at hand.

6. Aim to come to a point where you and the teacher are on the same page, working on solutions together for the benefit of the child – come to the discussion with suggested solutions rather than just the problem, adopting a proactive rather than a reactive approach. If the teacher or school disagrees with your suggestions for improvement, you may need further conversations or you may need to come to a compromise. Bring your funds of parent knowledge to the attention of the teacher so you can work together on strategies for improvement.

7. Avoid confrontational language or unnecessary conflict. You and your child's teacher are a team and you need to work together to support your child. Children should be at the centre of decision making in every case. Healthy disagreement is fine as long as you can keep calm, discuss options, and listen to each other's perspectives. If you can't come to an agreement, then you will need to make a decision as to what your next steps might be.

8. Once you've come to an understanding of the problem and have developed some solutions, make a plan to keep in contact and work through the solutions and goals together, to monitor your child's progress and make sure they are improving. You may need to have several meetings so you can support your child's learning progress depending on your situation.

Advocating for a neurodiverse child

There are many children attending mainstream schools who have been identified as having neurodiverse conditions such as autism, ADHD, ADD, dyslexia, and other learning challenges.

Learning challenges can be identified when behaviour such as getting distracted easily, low motivation, inability to plan time for tasks, copying incorrectly or behavioural issues begin to appear. These behaviours do not necessarily warrant diagnosis of a learning difficulty, but they can be signs that a child is struggling with some of their learning or social skills.

Some children present with other learning challenges. The following information has been adapted from the Energia Structure of Intellect SOI Certified Learning Manual (2023):

1. Dyslexia (reading)

There are two types of learning challenges when it comes to reading:

- Difficulty grasping the association between letters of the alphabet, words and sounds
- Reading comprehension issues occur when a child has difficulty understanding the meaning of words, phrases, and paragraphs. Reading speed and fluency, letter and word recognition and understanding concepts.

2. Dysgraphia (writing)

Learning disabilities in writing can involve:

- Physical act of writing – forming words and letters
- Mental activity of comprehending

Expressive writing challenges indicate a struggle to organise thoughts on paper. They include issues with:

- Neatness in writing
- Copying of letters and words
- Spelling and writing organisation
- Saying words out loud while writing
- Leaving words incomplete when writing sentences.

3. Dyscalculia (numbers and mathematical concepts)

Learning challenges in mathematics differ depending on the child's other strengths and areas for improvement. A child's capacity to do numerical calculations will be affected differently by a language learning disability, or a visual disorder or difficulty with mental capacities such as sequencing, memory or organization. These may include:

- Difficulty with math-related word problems
- Problems with cash transactions

- Trouble recognizing logical information sequences
- Trouble with understanding the time sequence of events
- Difficulty with verbally describing mathematical processes.

If you suspect your child may have a learning challenge, you are encouraged to discuss this with their teachers or a learning leader at the school who knows your child.

I am not a parent of a neurodiverse child myself but my understanding of learning, the human brain and cognitive skills, and how these impact how we learn, has inspired me to understand how we learn and how I learn. I realised that some of the learning challenges I had as a child aligned with some of the challenges on this list. I believe that if I had been supported with early intervention for these challenges, I may not have struggled so much at school, particularly in maths.

As I was researching to write this book, I became interested to learn more about how parents are managing when it comes to supporting their children with additional learning challenges, or what is now termed as 'neurodiverse' learning needs, and how children are being supported in mainstream schools. I interviewed two parents who also work in education, supporting families and students through these challenges. Both have neurodiverse children and have had issues when it came to trying to support their children to "fit the mould" of the education environment they are navigating.

I asked one parent, Amanda, what parent engagement in learning looks like for children with neurodiverse or additional learning needs.

> Most parents know their children need help but are often at a loss as to how to go about it and who to contact. Unfortunately some schools also put blocks up without necessarily meaning to. In my experience, schools all differ in their approach in relation to neurodiverse students – some naturally are brilliant and others, not so good. Some only seem to want to (or perhaps are forced to) focus on those students that are funded whereas others will also include those with other challenges regardless of their funding situation. Some private and public schools are great and others might want to assist but don't seem to really know how to best go about it – those that tend to have dedicated learning support

staff are great and those that have teachers adding this to their workload are not always supported in the right way to be able to engage effectively with parents to support students.

Some of the negative experiences I've witnessed have included a reluctance to provide individual learning plans for students and just focusing on leaving it to the students to advocate for themselves. Naturally this isn't always going to happen as they can be anxious, self conscious and don't really know what they are able to ask for. This is why it's critical that parents are able to advocate on their behalf so they are not left to their own devices and floundering around trying to make it through school. Some schools will support their students no matter what, and others, sadly, are still reluctant.

I have been privileged to be able to support parents through the advocacy process and most schools have been engaging when I get in touch on behalf of a student and parent.

At the end of the day we should be working together as a team – schools, allied health professionals, parents etc. Collaboration is much better for a student than everyone doing their own thing to support the child as we all need to be on the same page and aligned with what is best for the child.

When advocating for her own child, Amanda utilised her experience in advocating for her students. She knew what questions to ask and how the school was able to offer support – unfortunately many parents are not in a similar position and may need further guidance and an invitation by the school to share their concerns and work together in partnership to be able to support the student.

Amanda is able to identify what works well, what doesn't work well and what is required to facilitate successful parental engagement between parents and teachers.

> I appreciate teachers are busy and I always thank them for their time. Personally I feel they are busy regardless of having to add in extra time to support students. In my experience the school my son attended was really good at communicating and assisting us through the journey we had been on recently. My son had challenges with school refusal and it was a tough journey for our

whole family. There was a lot of follow up though still on my behalf at times, and I was fortunate to know how to go about this and who to speak to. Many parents really don't know where to start and how to go about advocating for their children.

When it comes to what support is required for children with additional/neurodiverse needs both at home and at school, there is need for further training for teachers. Amanda says:

I feel that better understanding of children's needs and challenges and how they can be met rather than trying to force children to fit into the way things are done [is necessary]. It can be like fitting a square peg into a round hole sometimes. Why are we so sure that the process of the way things are currently done is the best process, when really we should be looking into a system that works for all children regardless of their needs.

We discovered through our research and conversations with the school, for our son there were options for his challenges, with virtual school now being available. This should be a choice that families can make for their child, rather than the local school not being able to support the needs of the students. The message here is there is usually a solution, but we have to work together to find it. Many parents need to have further support at home to assist their children, either because they don't know what tools or strategies to use to motivate their children or their child refuses to listen to them. Once they are teenagers it's very difficult to drag them out of bed to get them to school. There are deeper challenges to address but it's not helpful to point the finger of blame at anyone.

When it comes to supporting students with neurodiverse learning needs, Amanda suggests:

I think we need to look at inclusion for all and not operate on a model that tries to make all those with special needs conform to the culture of neurotypical kids. Schools tend to often look at the behaviour of the child rather than the reasons for it and what supports can be put in place to assist. As an advocate for your child, you know them better than anyone and need to ensure they are supported as best they can. I think as a society we need to continue to be accepting and accommodating of all as we are all equal at the end of the day. This needs continued education and research into best practice for all children and their learning needs, not only a model for neurotypical children.

In summary, the main points Amanda raised for parents to consider were:

- Discuss your child's learning needs with their teachers or the appropriate learning and teaching leader in the school to determine what extra support they may need.
- Don't ignore the signs or be afraid to advocate and speak up about any concerns about your child's learning needs.
- Explore what options are available so you are aware of what you are seeking for your child and whether the school is able to accommodate or negotiate ways to support the student.
- Seek further support if needed outside of the school but inform them of what support your child is receiving so everyone is on the same page.
- Always follow up after meetings to ensure your child is able to be supported.

Another parent I interviewed, named Chrissie, has two children who are neurodiverse learners. She has been on a mission to find a school that accepts and embraces them for who they are. The experiences she's had with her own children has provided her with the knowledge to help and inspire schools to embrace all children and their learning needs, and to work together with families to support each other through any challenges.

Chrissie cites the relationship between parents and teachers as critical when it comes to advocacy to overcome obstacles that children have at school and for parents themselves to be enabled to advocate on behalf of their child.

> Every child that comes into a classroom, for a teacher, is a privilege and the way education is shifting means we are going to see more and more neurodiverse children in mainstream settings and we have to evolve and grow. Success really comes back to respectful relationships – human connection. We are all human beings, teachers are doing the best they can, parents are doing the best they can and we have this beautiful little human being who is

caught in the middle. At the end of the day, we as adults have to develop a really respectful, open, honest dialogue about how we can support this child to grow and be the best human being they can be.

Through her journey with her children, Chrissie has had some challenges in helping educators to "understand that parents are a vital part of the success of our children." She goes on:

> We know everything about them. We know what works, we know their triggers, we understand their sensory needs, we are a vault of information and we are your allies, we are not a threat, we are here to work alongside you.
>
> I see the real block in education is that we've got these educators who are highly trained professionals, across pedagogy, learning styles, but they are not the expert in my child, I am.
>
> I am a mum who knows this kid inside and out. I am his number one champion and I am the one person on this planet who has to make noise and advocate for my own child – but I must do this in a positive, calm, connected way because we want teachers to become allies. We want schools and families to become a collective village where we are all working together for a great future for children.

Some parents can experience push-back or be blocked by the school. Chrissie states, "One of the things I have seen in my own experience and I know is happening in many schools, is parents being told by leadership, 'Don't tell us how to do our job; we know what is best for our students.'"

In other stories parents have shared with me, many are faced with having their children sent home from school and a reluctance by the school leadership to engage with parents to understand their child so they can work through solutions together in a calm and considered way. It then becomes a battleground, or parents end up having to leave the school to find an alternative solution.

Chrissie states:

> With the rate of children with additional needs presenting in our classrooms now, we have to get our head around the fact that melt downs and emotional dysregulation are a part of everyday life for children with additional needs. Autism, ADHD, sensory processing

disorder, anxiety – all of these kids come with complications around emotional regulation. Every time they have a big feeling we send them home, they are never given the opportunity to repair after rupture, to apologise and to learn how to come back from that and move on and turn their day around. There is a default to punishment and removal of children when they have a meltdown.

As a parent, you may have some concerns about your child's safety, especially if another child becomes aggressive or violent at school, which can sometimes occur. However, as Chrissie states, "Safety has to be paramount and we have to protect other kids, but the more we normalise and teach other children about neurodivergence, the less scared or overwhelmed they're going to be if a child has a meltdown because he (or she) is dysregulated."

One of your roles is to educate your children about the challenges other children may have. There are many types of neurodivergence, and all children will benefit from understanding how other people can be different from them – either by being neurotypical or having a different type of divergent brain. Talk to your children about how they can manage their own emotions when they witness certain behaviours at school. Working with the school to understand what is happening can help to improve your awareness of any challenges for teachers in the classroom and your responses to what your children may share.

Parents as decision makers and collaborators

As your child moves through school there are many and varied decisions you need to make that relate to their learning and development. You may notice when your child begins the school journey that many decisions about your child need to be handed over to the school. However, it is also worth understanding that there are shared decisions that need to be made by both the teacher/school staff and you as the child's parent.

> **Some examples of decision making and a collaborative approach are:**
> - Giving permission for school excursions, swimming programs, and being informed of other learning that may impact your child's wellbeing, such as sensitive topics – parents should be

given the opportunity to be informed and make a decision about whether the content is appropriate for their child. This is not always offered for parents but you can ask the school for more information if you have concerns.
- Collaborating with the teacher and your child on their learning goals so you are kept in the loop about what they are learning in real time and where they may need improving or further support – engagement can be enabled when parents are included as part of the team and are empowered to know how to support their child. The sooner parents know where they can give support, the sooner they can work on positive and constructive solutions with their children.
- Sharing your knowledge of your child with the teacher, and the teacher sharing their knowledge of your child as they are at school, is a collaborative teamwork approach to all being on the same page so decisions can be made with relevant information.
- Deciding whether your child is well or unwell enough to go to school or come home – as a parent in tune with your child, you can usually tell before others that your child is not well or if there are other issues causing them to feel unwell or wanting to come home.
- Deciding which friendships are healthy for your child and which are not, and how to help them navigate the ups and downs that are normal in every relationship.
- Supporting your child with decision making around subject choices and career pathways and engaging with teaching staff about these decisions in the senior years.

If you find you are struggling with decision making when it comes to the many things you are navigating, know that you're not alone. It's important to trust yourself or ask for help – whether it be a teacher, school leader, friend or family member – before deciding what you feel is best for your child.

Parents as data analysts

As your child moves through school, you will receive updates and data on their progress. Decisions will need to be made about what support they may need depending on how they are progressing. This can sometimes be challenging, especially if you're not sure what the expected learning aims are for each year level or how to analyse the information in their school reports.

Often your decisions may be based on perceptions or observations of your child and their behaviour both at home and at school. This is why it's critical that you ask questions of teachers about your child's progress so you have the data and an understanding of where they are now, where they are supposed to be and how you can both help them get there. This is a critical part of advocating for your child and making sure they are progressing rather than regressing, and for you to know where the gaps are in their learning.

Parents are not always fully informed of the process of learning and progress reports can be subjective and vague. I encourage you to ask questions, learn more about where your child is sitting currently and where they are heading.

If you are unsure of their progress, ask the teacher to share your child's learning goals and learning matrix so you are aware of learning expectations at various levels. If it is explained to you which level your child is at currently and the level they are aiming to reach, you will have a better understanding of their current learning progress. You and the teacher will then be able to discuss any extra learning you can do with your child at home that can assist them to grow and progress to the next level.

All of these examples demonstrate that parents and teachers have many specific roles and responsibilities to ensure they are working together to support children. There are many and varied roles that you as a parent have as you guide your children through their learning journey. It is important to recognise that many of these roles are in the home, not only based on school grounds, and the impact you can have on your children outside of the classroom is much broader than you may realise. If you are aware of these roles and work towards each of them as best you can, knowing that your guidance does impact your child's learning, they will benefit from the support you and their teachers provide.

Chapter 6

WELLBEING

> Parents have the greatest stake in their children's wellbeing and are invaluable partners for organizations striving to improve the lives of kids and families.
>
> ANNIE E CASEY FOUNDATION 2016

As humans we are experiencing change constantly; some children, as well as adults, struggle with change and the challenges change presents. As a parent, your connection with your child is so important as you navigate their formative years. It's also important to understand how to let go and allow them to develop resilience, while still guiding them as they navigate their education and all the changes that occur during this time.

As an engaged, aware and purposeful parent, you are also an observer. Watching, learning and listening to your children, tuning in and understanding them as people who are finding their way and their place in the world. In the previous chapter we explored the many roles you have to support learning, but your main role is to know and nurture your child as a whole person who has emotions, feelings, needs, and their own personality.

There are many changes that occur throughout our lives; physically, socially, emotionally, biologically and spiritually. Each one of these can bring about great change that we constantly need to adapt to and manage.

By the time your children reach the age of eighteen, they are considered adults. It is time for them to be more responsible for themselves as they embark on further study or their chosen careers. Adult children still need guidance and support, but most of the groundwork is laid during those formative years as young children – when as parents you are often at your busiest, raising a family and working. This is why good mental health and wellbeing practices are so important for both parents and children to learn, to provide the tools needed to manage as a fully functioning adult.

Your presence is a gift

> The strongest predictor of a child's wellbeing
> is a parent's self-understanding.
>
> DANIEL SIEGEL

The reason I explored your self awareness with a focus on your wellbeing at the beginning of this book is because when you become more mindful of your own behaviours and emotional responses, you realise how this impacts yourself and your own state of mind, and how this impacts those around you. Awareness of yourself helps you to face your true self and to make any changes needed. It can be daunting to look at yourself in the mirror, but often it is our children who force us to do this. Embracing this opportunity to truly know and work on yourself enables you to be more at peace in who you are, to be more aware of your internal self, and to be conscious of how your actions impact your children. You should never feel guilty about how you parent. You are still learning as you go and instead of worrying about what others think, when you focus on what you can control rather than what you can't, by focusing on your own self belief and self care, on your wellbeing, there are many benefits for you and your family.

When raising children and providing them with the best possible start in life, it's easy to lose sight of what is really important. Time is always a factor and having enough time to do everything you need each day can be quite a challenge. Spending quality time with your children gives you the opportunity for role modelling, for observing them and getting to know them as unique individuals. Parents who are in tune with their children and know them well have "bodied knowledge". Pushor says, "Parents know their children through sensory engagement with them; touching, holding, watching, listening, talking, caressing" (2020).

Knowing your children means you hold knowledge of what makes your child happy, how they behave at home, what their likes and dislikes are, what their true personality is, what upsets them and what calms them down, how they interact and solve problems and how they want to be loved. Parents also have "embodied knowledge" where our bodies become the "ultimate instruments of our knowledge construction as we know more than we can tell" (Pushor 2020).

There is often, but not always, a strong connection or bond between parent or carer and child – you can connect in more ways than you can imagine through intuitive and interoceptive connections.

An article published in *The Guardian* states "Interoception is the perception of sensations from inside the body and includes the perception of physical sensations related to internal organ function such as heartbeat, respiration, as well as the autonomic nervous system activity related to emotions" (Robson 2021). The article states that interoception is linked with our wellbeing. According to Prof Manos Tsakiris, a psychologist at Royal Holloway, University of London, "There's a constant communication dialogue between the brain and the viscera." Tsakiris also states, "We are seeing an exponential growth in interoceptive research," and "there's growing evidence that signals sent from our internal organs to the brain play a major role in regulating emotions and fending off anxiety and depression." In the same article, Dr Helen Weng at the University of California, San Francisco states, "Researchers and clinicians are recognising interoception as a key mechanism to mental and physical health, where understanding our body's signals helps us understand and regulate emotional and physical states" (Robson 2021).

Another way to describe the deep or conscious knowing you may have about your child is an innate knowing. Pushor (2020) describes this as being "abstract, non-rational, situated perhaps in the metaphysical."

It's important that you and your children understand that wellbeing is an essential aspect of life that needs to be prioritised every day. Focusing on wellbeing contributes to strengthening mental health and is a critical aspect of how you are able to manage through life's ups and downs. This is a focus in children's education and should also be a focus for every individual in your home. You can create a culture of wellbeing practices that provides a harmonious environment for everyone. We explored in Chapter 1 the need for your own self care. This also applies to children and you can lead by example and support them with their own self care routines.

When children are moving through different changes, their wellbeing – as well as your own – can be impacted. I recall a feeling of grieving when I went through many "letting go" moments with each of my children. Probably the most challenging one was when my youngest child was in year 5 and asked me not to walk with him to school anymore. He was keen to ride his bike and have the freedom and independence to get himself to school. I was hesitant for selfish reasons – I knew the time we spent together while walking was coming to an end. The conversations we had and the quality time spent together was now not as high a value for him as it was for me. I needed to let go and allow him to mature and take the next step in his growth. This was high on his values at the time and I needed to honour this and give him his independence. I then needed to find other ways to stay connected with him.

To get through this grieving process I needed to acknowledge my feelings and look at that moment from a different perspective. Instead of viewing it as a loss for me, it was a gain for him and his growth. I also gained more time in my day, but made it a priority to find moments to spend with him to stay connected. I reflected on my need to feel significant in his life, which is a strong value of mine. I needed to take some time for myself to get used to the idea that he may not need me as much now, but that he would need me in new and different ways as his life changed. This demonstrates how to focus on your wellbeing when changes occur with your children. You can allow this grieving process to take place as it helps you to let go and is part of how you heal when there are changes in your life. If you don't allow yourself to heal, you can become anxious or try to control or hold onto your child, which doesn't benefit them or allow them to grow as a person.

You may notice I talk a lot about values. One of the reasons we struggle in life, especially with our wellbeing, is that our values are not aligned with what's happening. If your highest values are not being met, this is when you can find life difficult or become anxious. The challenge is in knowing how to overcome the times when your values may need to shift or accommodate the values of others and their needs while also finding a way to meet your own needs. A shift in perspective is required so that you can release the need to hold on, to control or resist change.

This example with my son is one of many similar experiences you may encounter as you take on this role to guide your child through their learning. In a webinar I run for parents to help them to find a sense of calm, I explore with them what the main concerns are as they guide their children through school. You may notice that many of the answers relate back to the parents themselves:

- Not having enough time for self
- Fatigue
- Remaining calm
- Filling your own cup to pour into others
- Short tempered
- Feeling unbalanced
- Understanding why children are unhappy.

These answers indicate the need to focus on each others' wellbeing, and to check in regularly and find ways to connect and find balance.

Time with your children is precious and life seems so fast paced for many people. Seizing brief moments in time and being in the moment with them is so rewarding and can help you to continue to bond and be in tune with them. In her breakthrough study in the book, *Ask The Children* (2000), Ellen Galinsky asked parents about spending time with their children. Many of them discussed the importance of being focussed while in the company of their children and not being distracted by other things. Many parents felt that their children deserved their complete attention and that this provided an extra sense of connection and a sense of belonging between them. These parents believed that truly focussing and being in the moment with them is more important than just doing things with them.

Children very quickly notice if you are not listening or when you are focussed on something other than them. Over many years, I worked out how to allow myself quality time with my children in between other priorities, but it's not always easy. I seek opportunities to connect whenever I can and to be fully with them in the moments we spend together. They soon let me know if they think I'm not listening or if I seem distracted.

Here are some suggestions for how to seize meaningful and precious moments with your children:

- **Sit with them** – it might sound simple but when your children are watching TV, if you can spare a few moments, sit and watch shows with them. Laugh and talk about what you are watching together. In doing this you will be able to ask them questions to gauge their understanding of the messages, characters, story and other valuable learning opportunities. This shows them you're interested in what they are doing and what they enjoy. Moments like these provide a sense of belonging and show that you value time with your children. Even if it's only a short time, every moment counts.

Sitting might also be at the kitchen bench while you cook or even asking them to help you cook so you can spend time together. It's during these moments you can connect, even if it's in silence. Silent presence matters just as much as talking.

- **Play games together** – you could try joining in with your children to play an online game or board games. Through your interactions they have the chance to see another side to you, and often these games involve conversations, laughter and learning how to win and lose.
- **Engage in learning** – sit with your children when they are doing homework; share in conversations about what they are learning at school or tell a story about your own experience at school. Ask them to teach you about what they are doing but avoid comparing their way of learning with yours and the way you were taught. It may be quite different now and it's good to learn this from them. It also helps them to be aware of how much they are learning and growing. You can help by encouraging them to feel proud of themselves. Positive reinforcement gives them the confidence to keep going.
- **Eat meals together** – when your family is able to eat a meal together to talk and share experiences, this gives you a chance to hear and observe your children. It also provides an opportunity to ask them about different things they are doing at school or with their friends. Even if you only get short answers, at least you've had a chance to connect.
- **Car talk** – when taking children to and from school or sporting events, this is an opportunity to connect. I have found this connection more difficult now that phones are a constant companion, but in a car you can take the opportunity to ask questions or have a conversation to check in with your child.

There is a fundamental need for us as their parents to slow down, to make time, to truly be present and listen, to not worry so much about time and to just connect with them, listen to what they tell you and let them know they can come to you whenever they need to talk.

Why do we need to focus on wellbeing?

A person's wellbeing stems from how they think and feel, through bodily responses or emotions about themselves. Wellbeing is also connected with what the brain is perceiving and responses to what is happening externally and internally.

In his article on interoception in *The Guardian* (2021), Robson noted Prof Antonio Damasio's 1990 proposal that:

> emotional events begin with non-conscious changes in bodily states, called "somatic markers": when you see an angry dog, for instance, and your muscles tense or your heart begins to race. This physiological reaction occurs before you are even aware of the emotion, and it is only when the brain detects the alteration to the body's internal state, through interoception, that we actually experience the feeling and allow it to shape our behaviour. Without the back-and-forth between the brain and the body, the feelings of happiness, sadness or excitement wouldn't exist.

In our fast-paced, ever-changing world, skills to manage this back and forth between the brain and the body and the ability to cope through the many changes in our daily lives are essential for having a healthy mind and body. Every aspect of your life influences your state of wellbeing. The Better Health Channel of the Victorian Government (2021) lists the following factors as enhancing a person's wellbeing:

- Happy and intimate relationships
- Network of close friends
- Enjoyable and fulfilling career
- Enough money
- Regular exercise
- Nutritious diet
- Enough sleep
- Spiritual or religious beliefs
- Fun hobbies and leisure pursuits

- Healthy self-esteem
- Optimistic outlook
- Realistic and achievable goals
- Sense of purpose and meaning
- A sense of belonging
- The ability to adapt to change
- Living in a fair and democratic society.

While it is aspirational to want to achieve these, many of the factors listed need certain guidance and knowledge in how to achieve them. This takes time, intentional focus and commitment, as well as the willingness to explore each of them as a part of daily life.

Contributing factors for healthy wellbeing

There are several factors that contribute to healthy wellbeing, and these don't always come naturally. Many of them need to be taught and modelled and are a work in progress over every person's lifetime.

In terms 3 and 4 of 2021, Buckley Flack et al. undertook a wellbeing pilot survey of fifty-two schools in Australia, New Zealand, Singapore and Vietnam. Of the participating students, 59 per cent identified as female and 41 per cent as male, with 42 per cent from primary schools and 58 per cent from secondary schools. The study found that the children were struggling the most with resilience, followed by their sense of belonging and their sense of safety.

- **Resilience includes** – developing skills of perseverance and not giving up when things get difficult; having grit and a certain attitude in how you approach life with positivity, passion, and a growth mindset; knowing who you are and understanding your own value as a person. Much of this stems back to how the brain receives and processes information, then how the body reacts and how the person responds as we've explored throughout the book.
- **Belonging includes** – healthy relationships with peers, family, community; school connectedness; trusted people to turn to who are good role models.
- **Safety includes** – emotional, physical, and online safety; respect for diversity; a safe environment in the home, in the community and at school.

Three priorities you can focus on when it comes to supporting children's resilience, belonging and safety are:

1. Modelling behaviours
2. Protective behaviours
3. Emotional regulation.

Modelling behaviours

When it comes to resilience, how you manage your emotions through difficult times provides children with a roadmap of how to respond in similar situations. In a study by the Canadian Institute of Health Research (Fleming & Robert 2008), resilience is defined as "positive adaptation despite adversity or, in more simple terms, how we bounce back after disappointment or when challenged." The initial focus of the research was the "invulnerable or invincible child, but psychologists began to recognize that much of what seems to promote resilience originates outside of the individual."

Research by the Resilience Project (2022) has indicated that significant numbers of people are struggling with resilience and mental health issues:

- 1 in 4 adolescents have a mental illness.
- 1 in 7 primary schools kids have a mental illness.
- 1 in 5 adults will experience mental ill-health throughout the year.
- 65% of adolescents do not seek help for mental illness.

A longitudinal study of Australian children released in 2018 indicated that, "a person's resilience is determined by a variety of factors, including individual, biological and psychological characteristics, relationships with family and peers, and environmental influences such as those in the school and broader community" (Evans-Whipp & Gasser, 2018).

Therefore, areas you can focus on to support your child to develop resilience are:

- Demonstrating how you respond to challenges or disappointment in a calm and considered way rather than over dramatising or catastrophising.
- Supporting your child's strengths and helping them feel optimistic about their abilities.

- Creating safe spaces for learning and relaxing.
- Surrounding your children with positive influences and being discerning about where they play sport, go to school and who they spend time with.
- Developing life skills such as interactive communication, building rapport, decision making, considering different perspectives, self awareness, empathy and coping skills.
- Encouraging healthy relationships with siblings, peers and family.
- Practicing daily habits to encourage and promote resilience.

To support your child in demonstrating responses to challenges, consider the following:

> If a situation arises with your child that they feel is unfair, how you react and respond demonstrates to your child how they might respond in a similar situation.
>
> Do you respond:
>
> - Impulsively with anger and frustration?
> - Instinctively through being protective? or
> - Rationally and intuitively? Assessing a situation for what it is, what the lesson to be learned is and how to respond to find a solution. How you show your child ways to respond or react and how to be resilient in that moment will assist their own resilience?

When it comes to reacting to something that may make you feel sad, out of control or anxious, there are always choices. You can choose to focus on the thoughts and feelings occurring at that time, then to respond with an action that demonstrates you're able to manage the challenge.

Whether you realise it or not you are always in control of your thoughts, feelings and actions. This is a really important lesson to teach your children as a way to manage their responses to what is happening to them and to build their resilience. When a thought comes into your mind, when you are practiced at observing your thoughts, you can stop it before it becomes a feeling that leads to an action or impulsive reaction.

Think about a large train station. All the trains coming in and out of the station are like the thoughts coming in and out of your mind. Some of the trains or thoughts are good ones, some are leading you down a line that is not going to end well. If a negative thought comes into the mind, or the train comes into the station, you can choose to get on that train and keep going down the line of negative thinking. The alternative is to stay on the platform, stand steady and grounded and consider how to proceed. You can choose to wait for the next train with the opposite or more positive thought.

To avoid catastrophising or experiencing irrational thoughts, instead of focusing on the "what ifs", or the fear of what might happen, think of what you actually want to happen. You may even like to visualise what you would like to happen rather than what you don't want. Thoughts are illusions, often created through false perceptions and thoughts about the past and the future. Some of the perceptions we have may be influenced by people around us. If there are other people in you or your child's life who catastrophise or create drama, perhaps discuss with your child ways they can manage their emotions when they are around that person or avoid spending too much time with that person.

Teaching your child that their emotions are important to feel and acknowledge, but that they can choose how they want to respond to a situation, can assist them to develop self awareness and strengthen their resilience.

Supporting strengths

Resilience is also learned by your children through your ability to let go and allow them to take on challenges or learn new skills without having to step in and solve things for them.

One way to develop resilience in your child is to focus on their strengths. In her book, *The Strength Switch* (2017), Dr Lea Waters outlines strengths that you should encourage in children:

- Positive qualities that energise us, that we perform well and choose often.
- Strengths used in productive ways to contribute to our goals and development built over time through our innate ability and dedicated effort.
- Qualities recognised by others as praiseworthy and that contribute positively to the lives of others.

When children are provided opportunities to explore their strengths, they develop self confidence and are able to see how far they can stretch themselves. Your encouragement for them to persevere and not give up allows them to build resilience, to fall down and get back up again, to bounce back from challenges. It takes patience, awareness and observation of your child to understand their strengths, when to push them beyond what they feel they are capable of and when to let them reach the next level in their own time.

Some of your child's highest values will most likely be different to yours. They may enjoy different sports, foods, entertainment and have other interests that you don't necessarily enjoy or agree with. But if that is what they value and if they are excelling in areas they are passionate about, one of your roles is to support their strengths and encourage them.

Much of what we are good at, or what can be seen as our strengths, stems from what we value most in regard to strengthening relationships, physical and mental health, spirituality, finances, lifestyle and interests.

In 2017 I attended and presented at the ARACY National Parent Engagement Conference. While watching some keynote presentations, I witnessed a talk delivered by Australian Olympic marathon runner, Steve Monaghetti. He talked about his parents' unwavering support for whatever sport he chose to take on. He shared that as a young boy he wanted to play football and even though he was a small-framed child and not really suited to football, his parents still supported him with his choice. As he got older, he realised football wasn't the sport for him and he took up running instead. His parents enabled him to find his strengths and encouraged him to discover what he was good at. Through the experience of playing football he realised he was much better at running. He loved running so much he went on to become an Olympic marathon champion and Commonwealth gold medallist, representing Australia several times across the globe. He credited his parents' support for whatever he chose to try and for their encouragement and focus on what energised him. Years later he found some scrap books his mum had made with photos of him playing football. It helped him realise the dedication it takes as a parent to support children's interests and all the lessons he was able to learn through those early experiences.

Sometimes your child may not recognise their own strengths but you may observe they are good at a particular skill. You can encourage your child to keep persevering and help them to see their strengths, especially if they try to talk themselves down. Sometimes children expect to be good at things quickly but it takes time and practice – they need to be reminded they are still learning and getting better each time they practice. Practice will strengthen their muscle memory, and that's when results can be achieved. If you remind children of this, they may be more interested in practicing and becoming better at whatever they are interested in to reach their full potential.

What do schools teach children about their wellbeing?

There are many frameworks, programs and strategies that are used in schools to help support children's wellbeing. In recent decades, science and research have uncovered many explanations about how the brain and body work simultaneously. These explain our responses to circumstances and stimuli, and help us understand why more people are experiencing wellbeing challenges than ever before.

If your child is learning different strategies to manage emotions and anxiety at school, it is beneficial for you to learn what those strategies are. This enables you to consistently support them at home.

Australian Schools Plus CEO, Rosemary Conn, shared in 2023, "Studies suggest a direct correlation between children's well-being and academic achievement." We know through research that children's learning is significantly impacted by their wellbeing:

> By Year 3, children with poor well-being are 6–9 months behind their peers and those from disadvantaged backgrounds are twice as likely to be affected. We know that targeted well-being initiatives can stop learning gaps from progressing as it helps them to get well enough to learn properly (Conn 2023).

This is why many schools are now integrating student wellbeing into the curriculum, but more needs to be done to support children. This is why it is so important for you as parents to support your child by understanding the early signs, knowing who to talk to about your child, reducing their stress and being mindful and proactive when it comes to their wellbeing. Considering the brain has to process so much information constantly, the content that children's brains are exposed to can cause them to feel like they are in a state of panic or on high alert. If the brain is taking in too much information, they can feel unsafe, which is when the primitive or protective (reflexive) brain kicks in. There is no room for rational or calm thinking when the brain is overstimulated with information that needs a rapid response.

The Australian Student Wellbeing Hub (2023) outlines five key components and how they relate to safety, wellbeing and learning. The components are:

- Leadership
- Inclusion
- Student voice
- Partnerships
- Support.

Leadership

In a school context, leadership responsibilities reside with school leaders and teachers to ensure a safe culture and a sense of belonging for all students in the school environment. In your home, you are the leader of creating a culture that ensures your child's wellbeing is a focus, that they have a sense of belonging within the family, that they are seen and heard and feel safe and loved. Part of your role as leader in the home is to 'check in' with your children and monitor or manage any challenges they may be experiencing, focusing on their strengths and supporting them with what they need, depending on their situation.

Leadership also requires collaboration. Your partner or other friends or family could support you in making decisions about how to support your child and their wellbeing. Consulting with specialist practitioners or counsellors, and collaborating with the school staff can provide you with access to support you and your child to find solutions to wellbeing challenges.

Inclusion

In a school context, this is the inclusion of active participants in building a welcoming school culture that values diversity, and fosters positive, respectful relationships. As a member of a school community, you can be actively involved in developing this along with the rest of the community. But it all starts in the home with how each person in the family is included in certain activities and decision making and how you are fostering positive and respectful relationships with each other within your family. This is part of encouraging healthy relationships with siblings, peers and family which are the grounding for understanding how to develop future positive relationships.

Inclusion means actively listening to your child and their needs when it comes to their mental health and wellbeing and working through important conversations about topics that they may be facing that sometimes may be out of alignment with your family values or issues you've never had to manage or discuss before.

Some of these topics may include:

- Online safety and gaming
- Pornography
- Respectful, healthy intimate relationships
- Sex and sexuality
- Smoking, vaping, drugs and alcohol
- Gender and identity
- Friendships and belonging
- Demands of school and study
- Bullying
- Social media
- Fear and anxiety
- Lack of exercise
- Healthy diet
- Sleep
- Lack of down time
- Self-esteem
- Pessimistic outlook
- Negative media influence
- Sense of purpose and meaning
- Resilience
- Self harm
- Eating disorders
- Ability to adapt to change
- Grief and loss
- Family or other trauma
- Scams
- Depression.

This is quite a long list but not every child will need to navigate each of these. If anything, you want to equip your children with skills to avoid, overcome or prevent these social issues. It is better to discuss them rather than try and shelter children from real issues that they may be exposed to. These are highlighted as examples of issues that can arise or impact their wellbeing. You can check in to monitor these and seek further help if needed.

Some of these topics can be quite challenging to manage or to discuss within a family so you may need to seek support if you are concerned about discussing any of them with your child. Reassure your children that they can share with you if they want to ask questions or seek any guidance around anything that is on their mind. This gives you opportunities to listen and understand how they are feeling, to enable you to work through any questions they may have or if they are feeling challenged and need further support.

Having a voice

Your child's voice, perspectives and opinions are important in your home culture and within the school culture. In a school context, this principle expects students to be active participants in their own learning and wellbeing, for them to feel connected and use their social and emotional skills to be respectful, resilient and safe.

The lessons children are learning from you are significant. It is the time that you spend interacting, listening and conversing that gives children an understanding of who you are. This in turn gives them a better chance to develop positive relationships with others. These conversations may sometimes involve debate and questioning, which should be encouraged to help your children think, solve problems, ask questions and be curious about the world and what is happening around them. Giving your child agency and a sense of self-worth to have their own opinions and views, as well as encouraging them to listen to others' opinions, are important character strengths to encourage.

Robust discussions about different topics, disagreements, and agreeing to disagree on certain things is normal and, if carried out respectfully, can be beneficial experiences for children. Listening to and learning from others is an essential skill to develop and helps children learn how to develop emotional intelligence. Truly listening and retaining information is not a skill that comes naturally to everyone. When children are able to listen, they gain knowledge, improve their vocabulary, retain what they hear and comprehend what you're saying. You can encourage them to understand other people's perspectives and form opinions of their own. It's important, then, for you to model good listening practices so children can become good listeners also. Encourage them also to listen to themselves and what their intuition is telling them.

My children often came home with questions about different beliefs and other topics they were learning about at school. I loved having these intellectual discussions with them as they prompted me to also question my own thoughts and wonderings about various concepts and beliefs. There may come a time when your children begin to question your family beliefs and values and it's possible they may choose to form their own. This may test you and how willing you are to be open to having these discussions.

Remember, you are raising an individual with their own views who will eventually go their own way. If they do come to you with a discussion about morals, values or beliefs and there is something you disagree with, having a conversation about it to understand their reasoning is important. This means you can understand their thought process, talk and reason with them about it and discover how to approach the situation. Sometimes all you can do to guide them is plant seeds for them to consider before making a decision, or share reasons for certain beliefs and values for them to think about, while also allowing them to have their own views.

Partnerships and support

When managing children's wellbeing, partnerships with your child's school, teachers and other professional practitioners may be necessary. Discuss with the school how they may be addressing some of the wellbeing challenges children are having through the curriculum or if they are able to provide further support for the students as well as parents. Many schools engage speakers and experts to share evidence-based strategies around many of these social challenges for children and it's important that you attend these events to learn how to manage at home.

Protective behaviours

Supporting healthy relationships

There is no doubt that your child's journey through school will be more fulfilling and happy if they establish a group of friends to share their experiences with. This is possibly the most difficult part of growing up and even as adults we can struggle to form friendships that are both healthy and thriving. Relationships impact our wellbeing in many ways as they are related to our core human needs and values of belonging, being appreciated and feeling a sense of purpose and safety.

In *The Whole Brain Child* (Siegel and Payne Bryson 2012), the authors share that strengthening relationships is critical to "...lay the groundwork for how they (children) relate to others for the rest of their lives. In other words, how well they'll be able to use their mindsight to participate in a 'we' and join others down the road, is based on the quality of their attachment relationships with their caregivers – including parents and grandparents, teachers, peers, and other influential people in their lives."

Supporting children with a strong focus on relationships and connection impacts children's sense of belonging, trust, safety and an understanding of the world around them.

Having already explored parental resilience, let's explore the social connections that you will no doubt need to navigate throughout your child's education journey. When it comes to your role in supporting your child's wellbeing and developing protective behaviours, a sense of belonging involves you also modelling and supporting healthy relationships and social connections with peers, family, community, and school. Helping your child form friendships will be one of the most common roles you have as they move through school and beyond.

So, what makes a good friend? How do you encourage your child to be a good friend to others and to seek people who will be good friends for them? What experiences are children going to have in a friendship?

- A good friend for your child is one who values your child's interests, is willing to give and receive equally, looks out for other people and has empathy, is courteous and who brings out positive qualities in your child that they may otherwise not display.
- In any relationship there will be ups and downs, good times and conflict. Conflict or differences of opinion often occur when one

person's values don't align with the other person, or when shadow values appear in the form of control, authority, rebelliousness, superiority and validation. Helping your child remain calm to make positive and considered choices when it comes to any conflicts, is an important part of their growth and learning.

- It's easy as a parent to say, "Just ignore them" when your child comes to you with a complaint about someone's behaviour towards them. Ignoring bad behaviour is a trap that many of us fall into. It can be detrimental particularly in adult relationships where one person has been conditioned to ignore the "red flags" (signs of an unhealthy relationship) and to "keep the peace" (avoid conflict). The relationship skills your children learn from you impacts how they resolve issues and recognise bad behaviour or red flags later on. You may need to reflect on this if you feel you need more support when it comes to conflict resolution. What are your children learning from you in how to solve issues in relationships and where might you need to be more mindful? Perhaps you could seek further advice around healthy and respectful relationships if you have any concerns about your child's choices.

- When it comes to relationships, developing good rapport is essential for communicating effectively, and communication is essential for healthy relationships. The various types of rapport provide confidence to interact with people of any age and can give your child the skills they need to operate effectively in the workplace and in social situations. You may like to revisit the different elements of developing rapport in Chapter 4 – Relationships.

- One of the challenges for children with online social connections is that non-verbal communication (i.e. body language) is often removed from the online experience. We're left to make assumptions or form perceptions based on emojis and shortened text communication. It's important to have conversations with your children about how to communicate and respond to verbal and in person interactions, and to share with them the skills of rapport building, listening and responding accordingly.

Friendships can be tricky to navigate and every child is different. Some are introverts and are perceived to be shy. Some are extroverts and love to be the centre of attention or the life of the party. Some are a combination of both in different social situations. Sometimes introverts are drawn to extroverts and vice versa as they see qualities in the other person that they may not have or may desire to have.

Being an introvert is not a negative. In her book *Quiet* (2013), Susan Cain states:

> Today's psychologists agree on several important points: for example that introverts and extroverts differ in the level of outside stimulation they need to function well. Introverts feel "just right" with less stimulation. Extroverts enjoy the extra bang that comes from activities like meeting new people.
>
> The introvert/extrovert divide is the most fundamental division of personality. And at least a third of us are on the introverted side. Without introverts we wouldn't have Apple products, the theory of relativity or Van Gogh's sunflowers. Yet recently extroverts have taken over. Sensitivity and seriousness are seen as undesirable.

Whatever your child's personality, they all have their own strengths and needs when it comes to functioning well. To be quiet and a deep thinker, to be observant and calm in approach is a strength. Many introverts are creative and critical thinkers, who spend time alone to access their internal thoughts and intuition that allows ideas and concepts to appear.

Your observations of your child's personality can help you to understand how to respond or approach them. It is reassuring for them to hear from you that they are enough, that they belong, no matter what their personality. If they are quiet and shy, and possibly clingy with you, enable them to work through this with gentle encouragement to take small steps to develop their confidence and focus on introversion as a strength.

If they are extroverted, this is also a strength. Try not to dim their spark and allow them to express themselves within the home so they feel safe to be themselves. It's possible, within the structures and rules of school life, that extroverted children may not feel safe to be themselves fully. If home is a safe place they can do this, all the more reason to help them feel they can be who they truly are. You may then take the opportunity to teach them that in some places or environments, they may need to stop and listen, cooperate and interact with others in a different way without losing their sense of self.

Create safe spaces for learning, sharing and relaxing

Another example of protective behaviours is to encourage children to know it's ok to ask questions and ask for help when they need it. Creating a safe environment at home for your children to ask questions or seek help means you will be able to support them in solving an issue or challenge, which in turn will build their resilience.

An example might be if your child comes and tells you about an incident that happened at school with another child who they didn't agree with. Instead of immediately putting forward your opinion, you can ask an open ended question such as:

"How did it make you feel?"

"How do you think that person should have behaved?"

"What would you have done differently?"

"Why?"

"What did you learn from this experience?"

This gives your child the opportunity to solve the challenge or think about it from another perspective before deciding how to respond, knowing that their opinion and views have been heard and are valued. This gives them the confidence to trust their own judgement and solve challenges themselves as they move towards adulthood. I like to call this process "planting seeds" – supporting your child to think for themselves based on small pieces of information you might provide, or a question that prompts them to think for a while then find a solution.

Emotional regulation

Another area of focus for children's wellbeing – and perhaps one that has become even more prevalent in today's society – is how to regulate and manage emotions.

In a podcast interview, Stanford University Neuroscience Professor Dr Andrew Huberman shared that the brain is either on alert or in a calm state, depending on the situation (Neuroscience Meets Psychology 2022). Often the body reacts without you needing to think about it (impulsive/reflexive response), which is an unconscious state of being. It's important to know how to manage emotions or feelings to cultivate a state of equilibrium (or calm) between the alert, but not panicked, and the calm state of mind. The body naturally feels good when it is in an alert but calm state. It feels anxious when it is in an alert and panicked state. To understand how to manage the brain, let's explore how you know when you are in an alert but calm state or when you are beginning to feel anxious or panicked.

Huberman shared the discovery of a new function of the part of the brain called the "insular". This is an important discovery as the insular is effectively responsible for interpreting bodily signals that send messages to the brain for movement or response. The insular cortex plays a critical role in interoceptive attention, which as we explored earlier in the book, is your body's way of letting you know something is affecting you. For example, when you feel hungry your stomach might feel empty or make a groaning noise to let you know. Or if you have been exercising and you get a pain in your side, that's a message being sent to you that part of your body is being impacted and it might be time to take a break. These alarm systems are essentially an indication that you may need to make a conscious decision (intuitive/responsive response) to change what you are doing so you come back to a state of calm, while also being alert or aware of what is happening to you in that moment. If hunger or the pain of a stitch become unbearable, a panicked state can set in.

Remember that you are in control of your thoughts, feelings and how you respond. When you are consciously aware of the insular part of the brain at work and recognise when those messages are occurring by the responses in your body, you are able to learn how and when to adjust your response to get back to that place of an alert but calm state. This can also be called being in a state of awareness, where you are fully in tune with your mind and your body.

Effectively, you are the coach of your own brain and you can train your brain to change how you think. It goes back to learning how to move from the primitive or instinctive/impulsive (reflexive) brain to the intuitive (reflective) brain by tricking the mind as the signal passes through the insular part of the brain. Instead of responding with the primitive or instinctive brain, you are able to reflect on thoughts, feelings and emotions before taking action. It is beneficial for children and for adults to learn these early intervention skills for self management of emotions and to shift how our thinking affects the body. Learning these skills does take time and practice every day and is not something that ever stops.

Through several years of coaching and learning about the brain, I have learned about another aspect of our personalities that is connected to feelings and emotions – shadow values are those feelings and qualities that were often squashed or dismissed as inappropriate when we were young. They are feelings that we seek because they feel good. Being prevented from having these feelings can mean we lose the confidence to be the person we are meant to be. Shadow values are related to the feelings and emotions that are attached to a person's behaviours. When exploring the concept of emotional regulation, the shadow values of seeking the feelings associated with attention, authority, belonging, control, rebellion, superiority and validation often come up.

These are all traits that children display in the family dynamic but also in their friendships. Children may seek attention when they are working out where they belong, who they can trust and what the boundaries are. They may value status, feeling special, standing out, being recognised and being praised. They may seek achievement, creativity, variety and fun. It is while seeking attention that children learn the boundaries of the family dynamics and how to behave in a society that holds certain values. We are often told that attention seeking is wrong but the feelings that people receive from that attention are what they value. This is possibly why some people like the spotlight or being a celebrity. If we didn't have entertainers who seek attention, we wouldn't have entertainment!

Children may also seek authority within a group or within the family. If your child has a dominant personality it may mean they value being in charge. That need for authority can be observed when children play or are forming friendships. One or two children may want to be the boss and take control of a game or make the rules for everyone to follow. While these are early signs of being a leader, children need to be guided in understanding that they also need to be fair to other children in a group. Encouraging leadership is a way to manage this value so that children learn how to assert their authority in a way that is considerate of others rather than dominating.

Similarly your child may seek control, especially if they are a perfectionist. They may have the desire to ensure they are in control of their world and can sometimes clash with others or have a meltdown to maintain or take back control. The need for control can occur if a child feels out of their depth or as if they might fail. Seeking control can come about in various ways, including aggression, dominating another person, or not seeing others' perspectives. If you recognise this in your child, you may need to help them understand what is causing them to feel out of control and show them that you can support them. The value of control is very common for people to seek, as we all want certainty in our lives. Unfortunately this is not always possible – a degree of uncertainty is a given in life and we need to teach our children to learn what they can and cannot control, to not be afraid to try and that it's part of learning when we make mistakes or fail.

Some of the shadow values overlap. Children may seek to rebel when they are denied what they want. If a parent says no, children can rebel to seek attention, control and authority – commonly seen as testing boundaries.

Other children seek validation to know that they are valued, wanted and loved, that they belong, and that they are doing well at school or other things they try.

It's important to set boundaries for what you believe is appropriate behaviour. Try to be in tune with your child's shadow values, recognising and validating them when they are behaving well and steering them in understanding that these values are a strength when used appropriately. If you are unsure how to set boundaries that are age appropriate for your child, I suggest consulting a developmental professional for further support or seeking resources that can help you with boundary setting.

It's important to allow children to safely express themselves in an authentic way, showing them how to respond and regulate their feelings. In their book *Anxious Kids: How Children Can Turn Their Anxiety Into Resilience* (2020), Dr Jodi Richardson and Michael Grose share some strategies for helping children to manage big emotions or anxiety:

- **Understand emotions** – these are keys to information about ourselves and are often signposts to teach us how to respond or stay safe (as I described in the example I shared about the insular cortex and interoceptive internal bodily feelings).
- **Tuning into emotions** – help your child understand the thoughts in their minds and how to make sense of them in relation to how they are feeling.
- **Check in** – check in with your child and teach them to check in with themselves, invite them to identify and express how they feel or felt

in a situation. "I feel this because..."; "I felt that way because..." then explore how they may respond.

- **Keep a journal** – encourage your child to record how they feel to remove built-up energy from their body and quieten their mind.
- **Practice deep breathing** – encourage your child to practice deep breathing exercises to release stress and energy.
- **Practice mindfulness** – catch those thoughts before they become feelings or before the brain responds in a chemical or mechanical way. Thoughts are not always true but can be presented for a reason – allowing analysis of thoughts means you are able to choose if the thought is worth pursuing or if it can be released (if you catch the train or wait at the station).
- **Encourage exercise** – it's good for the mind, body and spirit to exercise regularly and to release energy built up in the body as tension or pain. Exercise releases endorphins, creates mindfulness in motion, increases the chances of better sleep and reduces stress and anxiety.
- **Encourage plenty of sleep** – adequate sleep benefits growth hormone release and optimises learning.
- **Encourage drinking water and a healthy diet** – hydration and diet impact how the body functions which directly impacts the brain, overall health and therefore the ability to learn effectively.

Wellbeing is essential in how you are able to manage stress and challenges in your daily life. Monitoring your own wellbeing as well as the wellbeing of your children is a responsibility you shouldn't take lightly. There are many ways you can be nurturing daily wellbeing habits for you and for your family. If you are unsure how to support your child and you are worried about them or their behaviours, speak with a professional practitioner about your concerns so you are able to gain further tools to support their wellbeing. There are also many organisations focused on providing parents with the information and tools to support children. Know that you are not alone and that everyone needs to focus on their mental health and wellbeing to be able to thrive in life.

Chapter 7

WHAT IS PARENT ENGAGEMENT IN LEARNING?

> Parents, carers, and families are by far the most important influences in a child's life. Parents who take on a supportive role in their child's learning make a difference in improving achievement and behaviour.
>
> SCOTTISH SCHOOLS ACT 2006

When I first came across the terminology "involvement and engagement" of parents, I had never really thought that there was any other option than being both of those for each of my children from the moment they were born. I had never put a label on it and thought it was just a natural part of parenting. However, in the school environment, I quickly realised that there is a difference between the actions taken when you are involved in the school community and the impact on your child's academic and social potential when you are engaged in their learning. Both are very important in modelling and supporting children with their learning and development.

While working with and listening to parents, I have learned that many are very engaged in their children's lives and are guiding them the best they can with the resources they have available to them. Sometimes limited knowledge about schooling may prevent parents from supporting or guiding their children's learning effectively, depending on their own upbringing and experiences at school, and their broader family and other support networks.

You may already be doing many things in the home to support your children's learning and development without realising the specific impact on their learning at school. I believe all parents are capable of being involved and engaged in some capacity when they are more informed and enabled by the school, and by their children, to support learning.

As you learned in Chapter 5 – Roles and responsibilities, you have an extremely important role to play, but you may not have been encouraged or advised by teachers of the importance of providing your child with further opportunities to achieve and do well at school. This is no-one's fault as there is still a lack of training for teachers in why and how to engage parents in learning. Parent engagement is not yet a fully integrated part of teaching in all schools. I am on a mission to change this, and you can play your part by encouraging this as part of your home and family culture, as well as your school community culture.

What is parent engagement?

The specific meaning of engagement is to occupy the attention or efforts of someone. To engage in learning is to give your attention to the learning process and to the growth and progress of your child, making an effort to support them, through your active participation and interest as they move through school. I have touched on many aspects of how you can engage in your child's learning, wellbeing, growth and development throughout the book, but in the next two chapters we will explore specifically academic learning and the impact you as a parent can have in supporting this learning at home.

Through the engagement process, there are multiple people who need to agree to form a circle of support for the child and their learning. Each person must commit to working together to enable the child to reach their full academic learning potential. This circle may be made up of the teacher, a parent or parents, a carer or guardian, a sibling, a specific school staff member or learning support team, a medical specialist who may be working with the child outside of school, a wellbeing leader, other specialist staff or extended family.

The Australian Research Alliance for Children and Youth (ARACY) defines parent and family engagement in learning as:

> the capacity of families, in partnership with schools, to support student learning and achievement by promoting interactions with children and young people that nurture positive attitudes towards learning, confidence as learners, and the development of subjective learning resources. (Barker & Harris 2020)

The definition of parent engagement in learning at home in Scotland, where there is an Act of Parliament specifically for parent engagement – *Scottish Schools (Parental Involvement) Act 2006* – emphasises parents as the first and ongoing educators of their own children. As such, parents should receive information and support from school to develop their child's learning at home and in the community.

The Scottish Schools Act recognises the vital role that parents play in supporting their children's learning, by strengthening the framework for supporting parental engagement in school education. Scottish Ministers and education authorities have a duty to promote the involvement and engagement of parents in children's education. It aims to help parents be:

- Involved and engaged in their children's education and learning
- Welcomed as an active participant in the life of the school or setting
- Encouraged to express their views on school education generally

Parent Zone Scotland (2022) describes how the curriculum promotes schools and parents working together to improve learning and education and to encourage all children to become:

- Successful learners
- Confident individuals
- Responsible citizens
- Effective contributors.

I have often seen opinions shared in the media that parents are overly engaged and involved to the point of possibly stifling children's independence. However, in *Engaging Parents in Raising Achievement; Do Parents Know They Matter?*, Harris and Goodall (2008) state, "Young people told us of the importance they place on independence. However, they also reiterated – strongly – the need they felt for parental guidance and interest."

In 2019, Monash University's Melissa Barnes, Katrina Tour and Robyn Babaeff shared their insights from a study of diverse families and how they engage in learning. It stated:

> There are various organisations around the world promoting parent engagement, including Save the Children who deliver programs such as FAST – Family And Schools Together, to support parents with parenting skills to ensure their children are meeting the developmental milestones and behaviours for attending school and thriving in their learning. The focus is on supporting families, particularly with so many challenges in our world today, to be able to acknowledge and recognise the capacity to actively participate in and support children's learning.

Two parent engagement researchers and specialists I have learned from over many years, Dr Karen Mapp and Anne Henderson, share another definition of parent engagement in their book, *Everyone Wins! The Evidence for Family-School Partnerships & Implications for Practice* (2022).

> A full, equal and equitable partnership among families, educators, and community partners to promote children's learning and development, from birth through college and career.

All this evidence and more indicates the importance of your role in engaging in your children's learning. What does this mean exactly for you and what does it involve?

Engagement for parents is being available for your child and actively understanding their learning development and growth. This means knowing their strengths – how they learn, what they are learning and where they need further support to improve. This understanding needs to be in alignment with and include the professional advice of teachers, to enable you to seek support and enable opportunities at home to enhance the skills needed for your child's specific learning needs. Engagement is also knowing when to assist and when to step back, supporting children to become independent learners, to experience mistakes as well as successes.

Engagement means being willing and ready to listen and respond when your child is ready to talk, giving them agency to raise questions. To be engaged requires you to be fully present to provide considered responses or seek further information or advice from your child or from the school on their behalf.

Engagement means being aware of your role in facilitating learning opportunities at home, which provide children with necessary skills to enable them to learn, socialise and manage themselves more effectively at school.

Supporting and engaging in children's learning may come naturally to some parents but there are many who are unaware of what support to provide. One of the most challenging exercises for parents can be making the connections between learning at school and at home and how to engage in a way that impacts their child's academic learning. This requires a partnership between the school and parents that includes the ability and intention of the school to communicate learning that children are currently undertaking and providing necessary resources and support for parents to enable them to engage in the academic process. To effectively build the capacity of parents to engage in learning means teachers can be providing simple activities, conversation starters, games and other resources that enable parents to support their children's specific learning goals.

Research worldwide over the past fifty years has established a direct link between the engagement of parents in their children's learning at home and their children's achievements at school. Many longitudinal studies have been completed across the globe, including one highlighted in the 2021 publication, *Collaborating to transform and improve education systems – A playbook for family-school engagement.*

> In one longitudinal study across 200 public elementary schools in Chicago (Byrk, 2010), researchers identified five key supports that together determined whether schools could substantially improve students' reading and math scores: school leadership, family and community engagement, education personnel capacity, school learning climate, and instructional guidance. Crucially, schools improved most when all five supports were present. A sustained weakness in even one of these elements led schools to stagnate, showing little improvement (Winthrop et al. 2024).

In the same publication, communication of learning was identified as a critical element of engagement that is a cost effective way to increase engagement at home. Robust family engagement, as a core pillar of improving schools, certainly requires investment to shift mindsets and behaviours, but one particular component of this effort – direct communication with families – is a highly cost-effective way of improving student attendance and learning outcomes (Winthrop et al. 2021).

Learning is happening everywhere and there are opportunities available for children to be more supported by the largest network of people available to educators – parents. The concept of learning anytime, anywhere was established through a report released by The Harvard Family Research Project. Established in 1983, The Harvard Family Research Project, re-established as the Global Family Research Project in 2017, has served as a national platform for forward-thinking perspectives on family and community engagement research, practices, policies, and strategies. The 2014 report, "Family Engagement in Anytime Anywhere Learning" (Caspe and Lopez), highlighted the need to "broaden our notion of family engagement and of learning beyond school. We know that educational policy does not provide incentives for anywhere, anytime learning yet. It is at the community level and through private funds that we are seeing efforts to connect resources."

The report emphasised the need to support educators to look beyond the school learning environment into how families can facilitate learning anytime and anywhere using the skills and resources available to them within their family and the broader community. The report was also designed to highlight that more funding is required to provide these outside school learning opportunities for children of lower socio-economic status:

> We also know from research and evaluations from several fields that learning experiences outside of K–12 schooling help children get the skills and experiences they need to develop to be successful in school and life. For example, more time spent in afterschool activities during the elementary school years is linked to academic success, fewer behavior problems, and higher self-esteem. Consistent participation in afterschool programs narrows the math achievement gap and is associated with better work habits among students and gains in their self-efficacy (Caspe and Lopez 2014).

Other terminology used to describe essential learning to enhance academic outcomes outside of school were described in the report as, "complementary learning; connected learning; learning ecology; anywhere, anytime learning – all capture this constellation of expanded educational spaces and resources. Beyond the labels, the terms share a common viewpoint: Children from even the youngest age can thrive when they participate in a network of learning opportunities – in and out of school – that meets their interests and needs."

The report's definitions of learning in and outside of school clarified for me that parent engagement is essential for children's academic learning to improve. How this is implemented by teachers and parents to have an impact on children's outcomes is still a challenge.

Much of the research and literature I have studied since 2010, when I shifted my career to focus on working in the field of parent engagement, has been trying to determine how schools can engage parents in learning and encourage them to provide these learning opportunities at home. Communication from teachers to parents is the link between academic learning and the impact that outside of school learning can have on children's results. Otherwise parents may miss the relevance of making an effort to engage in children's learning outside school.

Dr Janet Goodall's research article, "Leading for parental engagement: working towards partnership" (2018), explores the role of schools in

> understanding of the child/young person as being a part of a complex and interactive set of relationships. This understanding of the child is by no means new yet it often seems to be neglected in schools and by school leaders. School staff often act, and leaders lead, as if all that matters in their students' lives takes place within the school grounds, and that all significant learning happens within the classroom. It is clear that factors outside the school influence significantly affect learner outcomes.

Some of the strategies I have developed for schools include firstly getting to know the families in the community. Understanding who they are, where they are from, their family context, how many people in the family, how they view school, what they want for their child and how they want to receive communication. Asking questions helps school leaders and teachers get to know who is in the school community and how much they matter in the lives of the children being taught.

I then try to go deeper, to understand the children and their place in the family and in their community. Who do they interact with, what challenges are they facing, what interests or hobbies do they have and how are they engaged in their community? How can we engage their parents to enhance their learning at home? What would work in their family context? What specific learning abilities does the child need support with? What are they already doing at home and what more can they do to enhance learning for the child?

I then explore with schools how to communicate more effectively with families to understand how to reach them. I encourage schools to rethink, reframe and rename "homework" to "learning at home". This leads to opportunities for teachers and parents to co-design strategies that provide parents with the tools to engage in learning at home activities and have a pro-active role in their child's learning.

Many schools have now adopted new technologies to communicate with parents. This enables parents to have an insight into the classroom. However, the opportunity to build on this strategy is sometimes lost. While sharing information about what children are learning is a huge step forward for educators in understanding the need to inform parents, there is little or no communication with parents about how to use that information to engage and enhance learning opportunities for their children at home. If parents aren't specifically informed about where their child is positioned in relation to what they are learning, the engagement opportunity is lost. It becomes information giving and receiving but this isn't necessarily benefiting or developing the child's learning – it would seem that it's more about pleasing parents or a surface level way to 'engage' parents in learning. The impact is only felt if parents know how to use the information to enhance learning opportunities, to have meaningful and relevant conversations about the learning and if they are equipped with the right questions to ask at home about what is being presented to them via the apps.

Communication between school and home has certainly improved since I was at school, but there are still many opportunities for teachers to have more of an impact on children's specific learning goals by engaging parents more strategically and intentionally. As mentioned throughout this book, supporting children is a shared responsibility, and with both parent and teacher being more informed of the opportunities, it is hoped we will see further growth in knowledge and understanding of how to engage parents as partners to have an impact on the student at the centre. This book is intentionally written to inform you of your role to actively participate in this important aspect of your child's learning journey.

Despite numerous resources now available for schools to implement parent engagement practices, there are still many systemic and other challenges in providing intentional and impactful parent engagement strategies. Parent engagement specialists Dr Janet Goodall, Dr Joni Samples and Dr Stephen Constantino, and many others, have written guide books for teachers and parents with many examples of impactful parent engagement activities for parents. The challenges are many for teachers, with increased time and resourcing pressures and a global exodus of teachers and school leaders leaving the profession. Due to the demands of teaching children with so many diverse learning needs and the ever growing issues of funding and accountability from the government and parents, we are also seeing a decline in people entering the profession. This is becoming a global crisis for schools and it remains to be seen what the impact on education will be in the coming years.

In my own experience advocating for parent engagement and talking with members of parliament and education authorities, it is clear that there is still a widespread lack of awareness of the impact parents can and should have as partners with teachers. In some countries, educators are not resourcing parent engagement and governments are not designing policy or providing funding needed to be able to implement a strategic approach to support schools. It's time for parents to step up to the task of initiating relationships with teachers and being intentional about supporting children through their education. It's time to speak up and seek resources and ways to support learning at home that can enhance learning at school.

In 2022 the US Department of Education recognised the important role parents have in their children's education, launching the National Parents and Families Engagement Council. The announcement stated:

> We all share a vital concern for the future of our students, and our nation, regardless of our political, social, or cultural backgrounds. Parents and families have a critical role to play in building a brighter future for our kids and our communities – the Department has always tried to hear from as many parents as possible and to engage with them in the most meaningful and effective way.

The formation of the Council is a historic step forward for the family engagement field and for the many families who want to do what's right for children. This opportunity gives diverse parent voices a seat at the table, to inform equitable education policies. It also creates the space to address and advance systemic family and community engagement in education. The National Parents and Families Engagement Council is a significant step toward the US Department of Education deepening its own family and community engagement knowledge and practice to support families, schools, and communities across the country.

How parent engagement is implemented is an ongoing challenge, particularly for schools. As noted by ARACY, "there is still a gap in how this (parent engagement in learning) translates to effective practice in schools and school communities". (Barker & Harris 2020) Engagement is a shared responsibility between educators, parents and the child at the centre. As you have learned throughout the book, you have various roles as parent, starting with knowing your vision for your child's education, how you are going to manage change and the various transitions your child will go through. Then there is understanding your role when it comes to interacting with the school and developing relationships with teachers. You are exploring learning with your child and focused on their overall development and what you can do to support this at home. You have a responsibility to work with teachers to understand how your child is progressing and how you can effectively guide and support them at home.

There are many opportunities for parents at home to truly have an impact on learning at school. To support children more effectively in what they are learning at school, parents need to be enabled to support learning at home by teachers. This includes communicating learning goals and expectations and providing learning at home opportunities that have a purpose to support the child to achieve those goals. This is not suggesting that you as a parent need to be a teacher at home. You are a supporter of the learning rather than a teacher of the learning. Your input is designed to support what the teacher is trying to achieve in helping your child to reach their learning potential.

Funding of resources and information for parents is needed to enable the partnership between home and school to grow and be integrated into the teaching profession on a world scale. There are various projects and initiatives being developed to build resources for parents and teachers to be able to work together in partnership. In 2018 I was involved in developing a national parent engagement toolkit in one of my roles as a parent advocate for Catholic School Parents Australia. The Gearing Up For Parent Engagement in Learning Toolkit was launched at Parliament House in Canberra in 2019. It explores fundamental resources for schools and parents and continues to build on those resources to support engagement in learning.

In 2017, Australian researchers from Swinburne and Monash Universities conducted the Numeracy@Home project (Phillipson, Gervasoni & Sullivan). This project showed that disadvantaged families often have high aspirations for their children's education and try to successfully engage their children in early mathematical learning. Numeracy@Home responded to the debate that families are children's first mathematics educators and argued that supporting families with access to resources, knowledge, and confidence to engage mathematically with their young children during everyday interactions is key to early learning. Such family-based early interventions supported by positive family-educator partnerships have been shown to greatly enhance young children's early learning.

One of the ways I've seen this implemented in some of the schools I worked with were maths teachers taking the initiative to run maths information sessions with parents to demonstrate how to play different maths games at home that supported the concepts children were learning at school. Parents were then provided with maths bags that included the games to play at home. This was a proactive approach by teachers to connect current learning at school with learning at home, with the clear intention of enhancing student understanding of maths and developing the cognitive skills needed to raise achievement.

The active participation by parents to play the maths games with their children and provide feedback to the teachers was all that was needed at home. The teachers were then responsible for measuring the impact of this strategy through the children's growth in maths.

Parental engagement is a continuous process from the child's birth to adulthood – it doesn't end once children leave school. The roles of parents change over time and in my own experience as a parent and going through the school journey with each of my three children, I experienced different levels of involvement and engagement.

I first began as a parent helper in the classroom so I could have an insight into what the children were learning and how. I wanted to help other children, not just my own, but it did give me a closer look at what my daughter was learning, how she was managing herself in the classroom and how she was developing as a person. That experience gave me a chance to remain connected with my child. I was able to understand what she was sharing with me about school and ways that I could enhance her learning in the home and beyond.

It's important to remember the learning in Chapter 4 about the relationship between yourself and your child as you engage in their learning. Engagement doesn't mean that you have to be in the school, even though my experience in the classroom did help me to understand more about how children were taught and how they were learning. Depending on your situation, what you do with your children outside of school can still have a huge impact. The report by Higgins and Morley (2014), *Engaging Indigenous Parents in Their Children's Education*, describes how to engage Indigenous parents in learning. It states:

> despite the vast and growing quantity of literature about the importance of parental engagement 'in schools' there is little evidence to support the notion that it automatically yields positive academic outcomes. The literature emphasises parent-school engagement, but this might ignore the most significant relationship of the parent: that of supporting the child's education outside school.

Parent engagement in learning includes activities that involve advocating and negotiating on behalf of children, as we explored in Chapter 5 – Roles and responsibilities. This may look different for different cultures, and as parents you may need guidance in how to approach the school to ask questions and seek opportunities for your child. In the case of Indigenous communities and for other diverse families in school communities, "it is better to engage in dialogue with the community rather than just parents on their own" (Higgins & Morley 2014).

Community conversations in school communities may look like:
- Talking in a group about what parents expect for their children, what their hopes, dreams and aspirations are for their children as they journey through school, and how we can support each other to achieve these.
- Educating parents on the expectations of the education system and what support resources are available for parents to engage in learning and wellbeing at home.

- Education on culturally safe school communities and how the school can support various cultural backgrounds and family contexts – knowing the children's family cultural background has significant impact on the teacher-child relationship and understanding of every child's needs.
- Role playing interpersonal communication through storytelling – keeping it less formal and inviting stories to be shared to have an understanding of families and their culture through storytelling.
- Ongoing feedback for parents to take steps to engage with educators – breaking down any barriers or fears of communicating with teachers.
- Enabling and helping parents feel confident to ask questions
- Helping parents understand their various roles and ways to engage in their children's learning, starting with relevant conversations about learning.
- Some schools do home visits to get to know families and what their needs are so they can understand their students and how they learn, what their family capacity is to support them and to nurture a mutually respectful relationship.
- Invitations for parents to view student learning at art shows and other exhibitions, to learn from the students and to get to know others in the community.
- Some schools host family meals and other gatherings to share stories so people feel a sense of community and belonging, which also contributes to overall family and children's wellbeing.
- Many schools are aware of mistrust between home and school and so are interested in exploring ways to develop a new sense of trust and partnership to support families and their children. The result can often mean students are less likely to skip school and their overall learning begins to improve as they are supported.

Your school could consider enabling these dialogue sessions in the form of community conversations to encourage mutual understanding of each others' roles and responsibilities. Your willingness as a parent to initiate and participate in these conversations will help you and your children to work more effectively with the school to improve learning and development.

What does an engaged parent look like over time?

As your children grow older you may begin to feel you can no longer support them with academic learning. Perhaps what they are learning at school becomes more complex or your child may begin to push you away – what's important for your child is that you are in tune with what support they actually need at each age or year level.

Once your children reach secondary or senior level, your role changes, as does your relationship with them and their teachers. They will have many different teachers and it won't be as easy to connect with each of them. "It continues to be recognised in research that this is a period of role change for the parents as well for their children. The parents also need to develop new ways of engaging both with their adolescent and with the secondary school at this stage of education" (Shakhovskoy 2021). Continuing to be engaged does become challenging but communication with the school and with your child, and supporting them with their learning goals remains essential. Staying in touch with them is critical as they navigate so many new territories.

An engaged parent observes and understands the needs of their child. If you know that your child is often tired and is in no mood for homework when they come home from school, provide them with opportunities to relax and unwind and decide together when the best time might be to start their study. Remembering that a focus on their wellbeing plays a major role in their achievements at school and in their social life. Often, they may have to work around you and your work schedule, and other family time as well, so this needs to be a consideration to ensure your child's learning is a priority. Family life is hectic and you can either adjust to suit what is required or work out what works for your family.

An engaged parent is organised with schedules around sport, work, school, other socialising and general family outings. This makes it easier for families to manage what is happening for everyone each week and to provide a more calm environment at home. Helping your child in their ability to organise themselves is very beneficial for their growth. Also be mindful and aware of your child's assignments or study needs so you can allow time for them to meet deadlines and be focused on completing work for school. If you are going on a family outing on the weekend, make sure you ask your child if they have anything due early the following week so you can allow time for this as well as socialising. Always be mindful of their needs when it comes to getting their work done on time, meeting the expectations of their teachers and navigating the needs of the family.

An engaged parent provides rich learning experiences at home that enhance their child's strengths and provide them with opportunities to explore new passions. They provide feedback that is relevant, purposeful and useful. They have conversations with their children to point out learning experiences and to relate what they are learning at school with everyday experiences, occupations, activities or events, broadening the child's awareness of the opportunities around them.

Ultimately, being an engaged parent is about supporting and improving your child's learning and overall development. It helps to have a starting point, a goal to reach and some guidance from teachers to enable you to share your observations of improvements to see if strategies are having an impact and where your child may need further support. This may be related to your child's wellbeing, behaviour, or a specific area of their academic learning. As a result of engaging in learning, you may see a change in relationships between teacher and student, between yourself and the teacher, as well as a cultural shift in the whole school community, all of which benefits children. Most importantly you will be able to stay connected and nourish a positive relationship with your child as they grow and learn and continue to reach their potential.

In the next chapter we will explore other practical examples of how children learn and how you can support their learning abilities to improve through simple yet purposeful activities at home.

Chapter 8

HOW CAN YOU SUPPORT LEARNING

Education is not the filling of a pot but the lighting of a fire.

W.B. YEATS

To enhance your understanding of parent engagement and knowing how to support your child, I'd like to explore what learning actually is and what it means for you to know how your child learns. When you have an understanding of how they learn, it becomes easier to understand them, why certain learning engages them and why they may disengage or struggle in some areas.

We have explored how the brain makes neural connections that are important for learning. Everyone's brain is activating connections constantly, but every person learns differently. Effective teachers are able to deliver lessons or content in different ways to suit various learning styles. When you are guiding your child at home, you can also identify ways to effectively support them when you understand how they learn.

First, let's explore what learning is. During my time facilitating parent engagement action teams in schools, the parents and teachers in my teams explored what learning is through group sessions and brainstorming. Their answers, and ways that other parents support their children's learning may give you some insights about what learning means for you.

According to parents I have spoken to:

Learning is:

- New experiences and understanding
- Age appropriate
- Brain processing information and retaining it
- Growing and developing
- Acquisition of skills through experience (directed and incidental)
- Connections – making links and building on them
- Academic; social/emotional; physical
- Processing and understanding
- Critical thinking
- Retention
- Discipline
- A practice
- Knowing and understanding how "I" learn.

The experiences or feelings we have while learning are:

- Euphoria "Oh, this makes sense!"
- Empowerment
- Affected by the environment
- Persistence
- Frustration until things become clearer
- Curiosity
- Learning makes you feel good and opens doors
- Always learning regardless of age
- Had both positive and negative experiences – learned how to overcome negatives and turn them into positives
- Experiences are different for everyone depending on the time, ease, style of learning (formalised or not).

With the learning experiences or feelings in mind, I asked parents to explore what they wanted for their children's learning at school.

I want my child to achieve:

- Good, sound academic foundations – just like a house
- Respect and good manners/courtesy
- Emotional, mental and physical wellbeing
- Friendship and memories
- Confidence and good social skills
- Good work ethic
- Ability to deal with different situations, including conflict
- Preparation for higher learning/education
- Preparation for life (academic, social skills, emotional intelligence, personal skills)
- Self-management and self-discipline
- Ability to problem solve
- A love of learning
- Independence
- Empowerment in making choices
- Resilience
- Leadership skills and to be proactive
- Organisation and planning skills.

These were areas of learning expectations for their children at school and many of the answers indicate more than just academic learning. I also explored parents' understanding of their role to support learning at home.

My understanding of learning at home is:

- Homework
- Household chores/responsibilities
- Working together with our children – helping them with research
- Showing our children examples or skills
- Explaining
- Playing maths games together
- Maths homework
- Tutoring
- Extra-curricular activities – swimming, dancing, sport, language, music, etc

- Providing our children with experiences to learn from
- Having conversations with our children
- Encouraging children to have conversations and interactions with others
- Making homework individual or personalised – this would motivate them to do their homework
- Children need to learn the basics as they already have the technology.

These answers indicated various ways parents are already engaging or enhancing their children's learning at home. There is still an emphasis on homework, but also on providing learning that is teaching other skills through experiences, conversation and interactions.

As a result of this discussion about learning we then explored what has worked well for parents at home when it comes to supporting learning, and the information that the school provided to support parents to engage in learning at home.

What has worked well in our home and family context:
- Homework on technology
- Passion projects – personalised learning where child chooses their own topic or passion
- Reading books
- Visiting library
- Playing board games, card games, outdoor sports, going on family excursions
- Transferring maths skills to real life – putting learning in context
- Family time together – dad getting involved
- Helping children understand there are consequences if learning at home is not completed by a certain date – there are few extensions given in the real world so getting them used to deadlines is important
- Time management
- Helping children be organised, to plan their work and set out their work in a manner that flows well
- Extra time to do project work.

These answers revealed families supporting children with life skills they will need once they complete their schooling. Learning at home is initiated by parents to ensure children continue to stay on track with behaviours and create good habits that give them an advantage when it comes to cognitive, organisational and interpersonal skills.

We then explored how a teacher-parent partnership looks when supporting their child's learning.

Parents and teachers working together looks like:
- Not being afraid to approach the teacher
- Helping in the classroom
- Helpful to the teacher that you're working with
- Understanding what teachers do and what they are trying to achieve
- Understanding the teacher's expectations to support learning at home
- Being positive towards each other
- Meeting together regularly to discuss the progress of child – both academically and socially
- Building strong and positive relationships
- Talking, laughing, friendly and positive
- Working together to achieve a common goal.

These were positive signs that parents are interested in working in partnership with teachers to support their child. Finally, we explored why teachers and parents working together helps children to improve their learning.

Working alongside the teacher helps my child because:
- Children learn from role models
- Better communication leads to better understanding
- Children are able to see that teachers and parents can work together to achieve a common goal
- Children value their parents showing an interest in their learning by having a conversation with their teacher or attending school events. It makes the child more interested in their learning.

These group sessions uncovered the desire of parents to support learning and to be a key player in building the foundations for their children alongside teachers. The parents' responses indicate they know there are areas they have the capacity to support. The answers show that learning is always happening, no matter where children are; with every experience and opportunity provided for children, learning happens before your eyes. You have the choice to initiate and be intentional in how you engage in their learning to increase their chances to reach their full potential.

It's clear from the many group sessions I've either facilitated or participated in, that many parents have a good understanding of what they want for their children, what learning at home looks like for them in their family context, and why partnering with the teacher is valued. Exploring how children actually learn will enable you to support your child's learning even further and will help you connect the dots when it comes to understanding your child more deeply.

How children learn

To understand how we learn – or, more importantly, how your children learn – I'll now explore some of the theories of learning. Once you know how your child learns, it is easier to recognise what works for them when it comes to their learning style, their motivation for learning, how they receive and retain information and what may cause them to disengage. This is really important information to share with their teacher as part of your funds of parent knowledge, and it is another strategy in understanding how you can support their learning at home.

The concept of learning and how we learn had never really entered my mind until I became a parent and started on the school journey with my children. It wasn't until my children started school and I began teaching at Victoria University that my knowledge and awareness of different styles and types of learning was ignited.

As a facilitator teaching students in 2008, I was able to explore how students learn, why some methods were more engaging, and why some students became disinterested in learning. I explored different possibilities and ways of engaging the students, to provide learning experiences and opportunities that would resonate with each of them as individuals. This included information sharing with visuals, group discussions and activities, role play and games. Understanding different ways that people receive and process information is essential when teaching and for parenting.

This experience broadened my awareness of how many personalities and various types of learners there are in the classroom. I also came to realise that many of the students I was teaching struggled with basic literacy, presentation and interpersonal skills. This really concerned me as I realised some of the assignments I was setting for them were way beyond what they were capable of completing. It got me thinking about how these students had been able to move through school without the support they needed and how, as young adults, there were many gaps in their learning abilities.

During this time, I reflected on myself as a student, to put myself in their shoes so I could understand how to teach them in a way that would bring them up to the standard required for the course I was teaching. As a student, I was an introvert and very quiet, often afraid to express my opinion for fear of being seen as dumb or being humiliated. There were some students like this in my classes, others who would rather be somewhere else, and still others who were driven to succeed and put extra effort into their studies. Back then you either fit the mould of schooling or you struggled to get through to the end. You may have had teachers who went the extra mile to support you and maybe some children had parents who helped them at home. Many fell through the cracks and I felt that the students I was teaching had somehow been let down by the education system and perhaps their families. This experience in teaching gave me an appreciation for what school teachers are managing when it comes to facilitating learning for children who are all different, who come from different families, cultural backgrounds and life experiences, and who also have varied levels of learning abilities.

While there are many theories about what learning is and how we learn, I will share with you a snapshot of what I have learned from various sources.

There are three types of learning:
1. **Formalised** – facilitated in the form of a course or study class that leads to a certification.
2. **Non-formalised** – learning through activities or workshops that don't lead to certification.

3. **Informalised** – the lifelong process of acquiring information and knowledge.

Then there are basic learning styles:
- Auditory
- Visual
- Kinesthetic
- Auditory digital learners.

The process of learning looks like:
- Exploring our intellectual capabilities – linking information visually, through sounds and other senses to then apply what we've learned
- Enabling discovery through trial and error
- Learning by curiosity
- Learning through conditioning or getting used to different environments and situations
- Learning from others through observation and imitation
- Doing things to identify likes and dislikes
- Learning through outcomes or consequences
- Observations that provide insight into connections.

Having the courage to discover answers that no-one has thought of is what young children do best because they are not yet conditioned to think a certain way or to fear failure. Children have a unique view of the world and their ability to think differently, to form multiple connections and to solve problems needs to be encouraged at home as well as in their formal learning at school. They are full of wonder and curiosity and you can watch them as they learn, which is a magical experience. As you observe them, you may be able to identify their preferred style and process for learning.

Culture plays a major role in children's development and learning. There are many ways that culture forms a person; their values and beliefs, their strengths and areas they may need further support with. Culture begins in the families we are born into, the language spoken, the villages we come from and the environment in which we formally and informally learn. If you think about your own experiences with culture, you will recognise how environmental factors affect us along our journey. They can be contradictory, conflicting and sometimes confusing for children, or they can be inspiring and enable the flourishing of learning and growth.

The concept of learning and how we learn is influenced by the environments we are exposed to and our way of learning is dependent on many other factors, including what we are taught, how we are taught and how our brains function.

Learning is applied when a connection is made between past information stored in the brain and the present experience. This is how prior experience helps to develop new skills and knowledge. The influence past knowledge has on the succeeding experience is called transfer of learning. In the Energia Structure of Intellect training manual (2023), Cormier and Hagman (1987) define transfer of learning as the "application of skills and knowledge learned in one context being applied in another context".

The more researchers learn about how we learn through studies in neuroscience, the more we can understand how to enhance learning for children. In her whitepaper *The Neuroscience of Learning and Development*, CEO & Founder of BrainBiz Sylvia Vorhauser-Smith states,

> Every human is born with approximately 100 billion brain cells, or neurons. However, what is far from formed at birth and continues and changes throughout life, are the tens of thousands of connections that form between each one of these 100 billion neurons. One of the founders of modern neuroscience, Donald Hebb, showed that neurons that continued to activate each other in this way strengthened their connections, like a path through a forest. "Neurons that fire together wire together" became Hebb's Law and a fundamental principle to how we learn. In this way our brains develop neural networks that embed and store our learning. (2011)

Knowing this information means you are able to encourage opportunities for your child to create neural connections so they can access their experiences and knowledge when needed. Earlier in the book I talked about myelination when the brain forms a connection that is then sealed by a layer of myelin, ensuring the pathway is clear for the brain to recall a memory, such as a mathematical equation or formula. The trigger for the brain to access information may be a word or an experience, a colour or a visual representation. This trigger assists the brain to recall the information then transfer it to a task or activity that requires that piece of information.

The brain receives repetitive information, subsequently forming a layer of myelin each time a memory is recalled. Myelin wraps around each neural pathway to seal the connection, creating a clear pathway so the brain can recall the information at a faster rate. This is an effective way for children to learn but learning by memorising or repeating a task or habit is only one type of learning that can be applied to certain roles or subject areas. Practicing a musical instrument, dancing or using repetitive physical movements, practicing a sport or a song are examples of ways to strengthen muscle memory for clearer neural pathways in the brain. As stated in the article "How Musical Training Shapes the Adult Brain: Predispositions and Neuroplasticity":

> Learning to play a musical instrument is a complex task that integrates multiple sensory modalities and higher-order cognitive functions. Therefore, musical training is considered a useful framework for the research on training-induced neuroplasticity. The brain, as the source of behavior, adapts its architecture and functions to perform new tasks through processes broadly defined as neuroplasticity (Olszewska et al. 2021).

Once the brain is trained to recall the information it becomes second nature – it's almost as if you don't need to think about recalling information, it becomes an automatic response from the brain to carry out an action.

The trigger that activates the brain to perform an activity or action can occur in various ways.

Levitas and Hurst (2021) describe Jerome Bruner's three stages of cognitive representation as:

1. **Enactive learning** – representation of knowledge through actions.
2. **Iconic learning** – summarising learning through visual images.
3. **Symbolic representation** – using words to demonstrate knowledge and experiences.

It is interesting to explore the science behind learning as well as these concepts further as they indicate and explain certain behaviours as well as demonstrate the process of learning which can be extremely helpful for you to understand as you guide your children through their education and overall development.

Enactive learning

The concept of enactive learning involves absorbing and storing information that is retrieved through memory, and experiences where there is an action, an outcome and experimenting as part of the learning experience.

An example might be when a baby is learning how to throw or drop an item to make noise, they soon learn that the same action doesn't always produce the desired outcome. This is where they are learning what the result is or can be from their action and what response they can receive from others when they carry out that action. They are learning soft from hard, noise from no noise, and that if they want to produce a certain outcome, they need the right tool or action. They haven't yet mastered this skill but they explore and discover that their simple repeated actions produce an outcome.

Once they work out which action causes the outcome they are seeking, their brain makes the neural connections and stores them for recall when needed. This is also helpful for children when they are learning about danger or their own safety – if a child falls or trips, and you explain to them that they may need to slow down or be more careful next time, their brain will recognise that whatever they were doing that caused them to fall or trip will happen again if they do the same thing again. So next time they are climbing, they may be more careful as the brain recalls that previous experience. This is why it's important to allow children to fall over, get back up again, climb trees, go exploring on uneven terrain and take other risks, that you know are still fairly safe, to teach them about repeat patterns or behaviour and consequences of actions.

Another example is when a child discovers the impact that throwing an object has, and how they often use it to gain attention. Throwing food is one of the first ways children learn to use an action to achieve an outcome. If the parent or carer over-reacts to them throwing something on the floor, they see another outcome and can use this type of action to gain attention because they know it will cause a reaction. How we respond to a child's actions impacts what and how they learn – you might like to question whether the action is appropriate, are they being validated for it, and how should I respond so their brain recognises that action has a consequence.

They may try it again to see what happens, to see how you might react. They may stop once they realise it's not getting the response they are seeking or when you point out to them that there are consequences for their actions. All the while they are learning what they are capable of and forming connections in their brain. As an observant parent you are able to see this learning as part of their development and understand that it is all part of a natural progression as they grow.

Children continue to learn this way both at home and at school, and they will often seek validation for their actions. Many children thrive when they know there is a purpose for their learning. If they don't see an outcome they can lose interest or disengage. This can then impact their motivation to learn.

Putting learning into context for children – providing them with the steps or the stages their learning will follow – can help them understand the process and see their own progress. After extensive research, Laureate Professor John Hattie developed the teaching strategy, *Visible Learning: A Synthesis of Over 800 Meta-Analyses Relating to Achievement* (2008). This enables teachers to support and share progress of learning with students, and to demonstrate how it is leading them towards their end result. They are able to understand the reason or purpose for learning, receive regular feedback or validation as they learn and understand the outcome or what they are actually trying to achieve. It builds a story about the power of teachers, feedback, and a model of learning and understanding. This type of teaching can motivate children to be more engaged and thrive in their learning as they "…are provided with an attention to setting challenging learning intentions, being clear about what success means, and an attention to learning strategies for developing conceptual understanding about what teachers and students know and understand" (Hattie 2008).

Iconic learning

Bruner revealed in his research that the concept of iconic learning begins from the age of one to six years (Levitas & Hurst 2021). Iconic learning involves children expressing what they see internally, whether through a drawing or by being able to verbally express what they are thinking, seeing and feeling. This is a particularly important stage of their learning to be encouraged as they begin to understand their internal responses to their surroundings and what symbols mean, as their brains are making thousands of neural connections. It is at this stage of development that children begin to learn "right from wrong" from their parents, and you can observe this through their behaviour and responses to various environments.

The ability to visualise and transfer a summary of information into reality can demonstrate how a child is thinking or what their imagination is telling them. This is an essential cognitive skill they will use throughout their formal learning at school. They often express their thoughts through drawing their own interpretation of what something looks like or a representation of an object. These learners are able to visualise, so use of symbols and diagrams makes it easier for them to follow or understand information.

Symbolic learning

Jerome Bruner's research also states that children go through a symbolic stage from the age of seven, when information is stored in the form of a code or symbol (Levitas & Hurst 2021). The symbolic stage is when children begin to understand the concept of categories and how items are organised into single words such as dogs, horses, houses, clothes.

Even though there are multiple breeds of dogs and horses, different styles of houses and different types of clothes, we soon learn that single words can cover a range or group of items under one single category. These categories can then determine how we perceive things as our brains seek to place things in order and simplify connections.

Categorising allows the brain to be more organised and enables it to make connections quickly and easily. When a child sees a picture of a dog in a book and then sees a dog in real life, they are quickly able to see the connection and determine that it is a dog. They may not have learned the name of the dog or the specific breed yet, but they are able to recall that connection. During this stage of learning, the brain is processing things by category, such as words, numbers or mathematical symbols. If children are able to recall connections through categories, this is a strength in their learning and can help them with reading and identifying letters, words and objects.

Learning and the brain

It is important to recognise that all people learn differently. What some people pick up easily may take longer for others to grasp. It has been observed that some people acquire knowledge and skills faster than others (Payne & Tirre 1984). Certain people can acquire particular knowledge and skills that others cannot acquire with any amount of training or time. Such individual differences in learning are most commonly thought of as differences in intelligence.

Through my experience as a facilitator of learning, studying neuro-linguistic programming (NLP) and through coaching, I learned how to facilitate learning by understanding the different learning styles: visual, auditory and kinesthetic. These are important to consider in understanding how your child learns, as we explore Joseph Bogen's 4mat method for learning (McCarthy, Germain and Lippitt 2002).

The 4mat method for learning demonstrates four ways that people learn and how each way is connected to the left and right brain hemispheres. There are two sides of the brain accessing and transferring information through perception and processing. Most people use both sides of the brain but when it comes to learning, they may have a preference for one or the other or combinations of both.

When you are presented with information, your left brain will experience and conceptualise the information. The brain will absorb the messages coming through that then results in a feeling or an emotion. It will then filter or censor what is happening before you respond with an action.

The left brain also perceives through conceptualising information or translating the sensations and emotions into forms, ideas and language, then naming and placing it into a system. This relates back to Bruner's symbolic learning where the brain perceives then places information into a category or structure to make sense of it.

There is an interplay of brain responses happening, between the "feelings" of an experience and the "thinking" of conceptualising, which is crucial to the learning and communication process.

The right brain processes information through reflection and action. Through reflection, your brain transforms and intellectualises information using your own personal knowledge related to structure and organisation.

For example, when you meet someone and ask them what they do for a living, if they give you a simple answer such as "I'm a plumber," if you already know what a plumber does, your left brain can recall the experience or visualise what a plumber does and this will give you a feeling to then recognise and transfer the experience of the feeling into a category or "plumber". If a person says to you, "I'm a consultant," if the brain is not able to access an experience of what a consultant does or a feeling or visual related to a consultant, you may reflect on this and form your own idea of what it means. The brain may need further information to be able to process and place the information into a simplified form that the brain understands and is then able to recall.

Learning styles

So what does left and right brain learning look like in practice for your child? During my studies to become a learning facilitator and during my coaching training with Authentic Education, I learned about the following learning styles to help me understand how to identify different learners and engage more effectively with clients.

Most people operate with at least one or more of these learning styles, and often some styles are more dominant than others. You may recognise some of these learning styles in yourself as well as in your children.

Parents and teachers are capable of identifying each of these learning styles and representational systems in individuals, whether they be your own children or, if you are a teacher, your students. Understanding how to provide learning experiences that are relevant to how children receive and process information, instruction and feedback can help children to thrive in their learning.

As you read through the 4mat method learning styles below (adapted from Harvey 2018), see if you can identify any of the styles in your child as well as in yourself as a learner.

Type 1 learning style asks "Why?"
Experiencing meaning (visual learner)

Left brain actions are the transfer of information from "experiences" and "feelings". Type 1 learners are curious learners, often imaginative and contemplative as they experience learning. They are visual learners who like to spend time absorbing feelings and reflecting on what they are learning to connect the dots, seeking personal meaning and involvement or relevance. Their personal values are important as they make connections based on their values and can quickly turn off if they don't see the point in what they are learning or if they don't understand. They can be impatient, wanting to know why, and wanting to learn quickly.

Have you ever heard your child ask, "Why do I have to learn this?" This may be an indication they are seeking an explanation of how the learning is relevant, or they may need further explanation to understand what they are learning and why. For example, if you are trying to motivate your child to practice maths strategies, you may need to think of ways to make it relevant for them, how it relates to their values and how to make it fun. Remembering they respond to experiences and feelings so giving meaning to the task will spark a response once their values and learning needs are met.

Earlier in the book I mentioned my aversion to maths because of my humiliating experience in year 4. I equated maths with that experience and the feeling of humiliation ever since that day. I have therefore always struggled in maths and with remembering numbers. For me to learn about anything to do with maths now, I need to rewire my brain to not access those experiences and feelings anymore. I would need to change my story to a new experience and feelings when it comes to numbers, maths and money. The story embedded in my subconscious triggers a feeling of lack or humiliation which has a powerful impact on my relationship to this type of learning. This highlights how important "feelings" and "experiences" are when it comes to learning.

Visual learners are aware of their visual presentation and how they appear to others. This can be evident in the presentation of their work, taking great pride in making sure their work is visually appealing. In learning, they often use visual symbols, graphs or images to memorise information and to present ideas.

I am a very visual person and am able to remember landmarks more easily than street names. Working as a graphic designer for more than thirty years provided me with the ability to interpret structured information or words into visuals, to design a symbol that represents an idea or concept to communicate a message and a feeling for the viewer. To be able to do this I had to put myself in the shoes of the client or customer to visualise the experience and feelings they have when using a product or service so I could represent the information in a way that would appeal to that customer.

Visual learners may find it more difficult to recall information without visual cues or symbols. Receiving, retaining and memorising words or a lot of information at once can be a challenge. This is important to remember when your child is studying – if they are more visual, you can suggest they use cue cards or connect words with images as a way for them to remember facts and other information. The use of shapes or objects can help to trigger a memory of an experience or feeling – this is more successful for this type of learner than trying to remember verbal instructions or written sentences. Word association games, creating a visual movie in the mind or a visual story can help this type of learner memorise and recall information.

You can apply these strategies when teaching them how to remember instructions, how to be more organised, to provide experiences that appeal to their values and other ways to motivate them to learn or take action.

Type 2 learning style asks "What?"
Conceptualising ideas (auditory learner)

These are analytical learners who prefer facts, numbers and statistics, the opportunity to think through ideas and ask questions to clarify. These learners seek specifics and concrete answers or evidence from other experts. Their favourite question is "What?"

They are able to conceptualise when they are informed of the facts. They are left brain thinkers, usually auditory (good listeners) and able to retain information that is provided verbally.

If you have a child who is an auditory learner they may be a very good listener, able to learn by listening and easily memorising information. They may respond to tone of voice, particularly when receiving feedback verbally. Apart from listening they also like to talk and enjoy music. Stories and metaphors, case studies or testimonials are more likely to engage these learners.

Type 3 learning style asks "How?"
Applying skills (kinesthetic learners)

These are patient, common sense learners who like to think and take action. They are the implementers of the ideas. They are most happy experimenting, building and creating usability. They like to tinker and apply useful ideas. They are known as kinesthetic learners and right brain thinkers.

Kinesthetic people learn through their sense of touch. They like to work with their hands and enjoy physical rewards. They learn by doing, like to take action with activities to assist in memorising and remembering how to carry out a task. They also have to feel right about something before they go ahead with it. These learners may be restless and need activities to be able to fulfil their need to move and use their hands to create or complete a task. They are more likely to remember how to do something by actually doing it physically rather than being told or reading how to do it. They may need to be shown a task once and then enabled to actually do it (and repeat it) so they are able to recall how to do it.

Type 4 learning style asks "What if?"
Adaption (auditory digital learners)

These are dynamic learners who like doing and feeling. They can be described as auditory digital as they are seeking hidden possibilities and exploring ideas to create original adaptations. They often learn by trial and error and self discovery. Their favourite question is "'What if?". They are the innovators of the world who are not afraid to try things and figure out the answers.

Auditory digital learners are deep thinkers who listen to their internal messages or intuition, and want to explore alternatives to find solutions. They have the ability to use all of the above learning styles but often need certainty that what they are doing makes sense or they don't see the point in doing it. These learners require an explanation of why something is important and what the purpose of an activity is. They are more likely than other learning types to want to question, test a theory and experiment further.

Cognitive and non-cognitive learning skills

Cognitive skills enable you to interpret or comprehend the world around you. Cognitive abilities enable you to identify objects and their differences and similarities. Cognitive abilities provide the capacity to learn to speak, read, listen, touch, feel and interpret information. Decision making, the way you communicate, memorise information as well as how you form perceptions are all cognitive abilities and these stem from the nurturing of each of the learning styles we just explored.

Non-cognitive skills cover a range of abilities that involve social and emotional development where children are learning how to manage themselves, be motivated and able to work with others, such as conscientiousness, perseverance, and teamwork. These skills are critically important to student achievement, both in and beyond the classroom. They form a vital piece of workers' skill sets, which comprise cognitive, non-cognitive and job-specific skills.

These skills are learned from the time you are born but some children miss out on learning them if they are not encouraged to engage in various activities or experiences, including social interactions and learning through play. A lack or loss of cognitive abilities means some areas of learning are seriously impacted.

Cognitive and non-cognitive skills are "essential skills" because they provide the tools for children to learn effectively at school and to manage in daily life. These skills are required to perform functions across most professions, but they are also critical for learning and life skills in general.

Having a good understanding of our intellect, and the intellect of the people who we interact with, will help us to make better decisions for ourselves and also help us to understand why someone else does things differently.

To understand how we learn cognitive skills, I explored the Structure of Intellect Theory (1955) created by Joy Paul Guilford, a psychometrician who specialised in understanding human intelligence. "This theory is used in education to identify cognitive skills that are needed for effective learning. The Structure of Intellect provides a map of human intelligence. It charts the territory. It indicates the best method of getting to educational goals" (Energia 2023)

The following is adapted from Energia's Structure of Intellect (SOI) training (2023), which describes the theory and how formalised, non-formalised and informalised learning is applied.

1. **Operations** – how learning abilities are actioned or implemented.
2. **Content** – three types of intelligence in how information is received and interpreted by the learner.
3. **Products** – the complexity of the information or data being presented – information that is delivered that the learner must analyse and present in different ways to demonstrate understanding or to perform a task.

Operations include the following essential learning skills:
- **Cognition:** comprehension, recognition of information in various forms – visual, verbal/auditory, kinesthetic, auditory digital
- **Memory:** recall, interpretation of incidental information, listening to recall or paraphrase and interpret information that has been delivered
- **Evaluation:** making judgements, organisational skills, reasoning, decision making and foresight
- **Critical thinking:** finding a solution from the information that is provided – much like solving a puzzle or mystery. The information provides clues and then each of these pieces come together to find a solution using reasoning and logic
- **Creative thinking:** the use of information to create ideas that are flexible, the ability to think outside normal conditioning and then apply the idea in a structured and disciplined way to then be interpreted by others.

Content includes the three types of intelligence:
- **Figural:** sensory content that can be identified through touch, hearing and seeing. Concrete information such as symbols, shapes, sounds
- **Symbolic:** numbers and words based content, signs, letters, mathematics, time, musical notes, etc
- **Semantic:** understanding overall concepts and ideas through reading and interpretation of written words or visual information that has a message or concept that is being communicated.

The ideal measure of learning ability is a balance of understanding and interpreting all three of these content parameters.

Products include:
- Figural, symbolic and semantic **units:** recognising and interpreting one piece of information at a time

- Figural, symbolic and semantic **classes**: identifying groups or sets
- Figural, symbolic and semantic **relations**: associations between words or numbers, placement, symbols, opposites, comparisons in size, colour, shapes)
- Figural, symbolic and semantic **systems**: understanding sequences, connections and instructional information
- Figural, symbolic and semantic **transformations**: creativity; seeing and applying objects, shapes, designs, concepts from different perspectives
- Figural, symbolic and semantic **implications**: problem solving and decision making; ability to interpret facts and propositions to come to an outcome or conclusion.

It's possible to combine various skills at the same time – an example to support the improvement of your child's operational, content and product skills, is to give them instructions and observe how many of these they follow and how they interpret the information you give them. Take notice of the type of information you provide them, how they review it, make decisions and solve problems, and their ability to explain why they chose one solution over another.

A simple activity you can try (with children from the age of seven) that demonstrates a number of different cognitive skills is to ask your child to call a relative or friend to arrange a meet up or a meeting in person. In the list below, you will see the cognitive skills being learned and any other skills being applied. The operation, the type of content and the product applied with each skill are indicated in brackets.

Ask your child to make the phone or video call. Observe and listen to the conversation and then ask your child a few of the following questions (you don't have to ask them all but the following questions are ones that you can use at other times to help them develop their cognitive skills.

- What did you hear during your conversation? (listening skills, memory/recall)
- What information did they give you? (comprehension and interpretation of content)

- What questions did you ask them? (curiosity)
- What questions did they ask you? (memory recall and interpretation of content)
- What did you answer? (memory and evaluation)
- How did you know the answer? (memory and problem solving)
- What did you learn about them? (memory, comprehension and evaluation)
- What decisions did you make? (critical thinking and decision making)
- What plans did you make? (transformations and implications, evaluation, organisation/strategising/decision making)
- What made you decide that? (cognition, critical thinking and decision making)
- Was it your decision or theirs or both? (evaluation, co-operation/flexibility)
- What do you need to do to make your plans happen? (action taking/action steps/planning)
- How will you record and remember that information? (creative thinking)
- What will you do there? (evaluation – thinking ahead, foresight)
- What will you need to take? (operational critical thinking and decision making)
- How will you get there? (evaluation – thinking ahead, foresight)
- What will make the day enjoyable for you? (evaluation – thinking ahead, foresight)
- What will you do if plans change? (transformations and implications; being flexible, critical and creative thinking, having foresight, finding a solution to a potential problem).

A simple conversation on the phone can provide your child with exposure to and practice of skills to strengthen their cognitive learning abilities. If your child isn't able to carry out this task or answer these questions, it doesn't mean they don't have the requisite skills for learning but could highlight some areas you might like to work on improving with them.

To enable you to support your child's learning at home, here are some ideas you may like to try to encourage the left and right brain, enactive, iconic and symbolic learning as well as cognitive and non-cognitive skills:

Enactive learning at home

- Science experiments
- Cooking together
- Ball games
- Lego or building blocks
- Make slime
- Measure and make
- Observation games that lead to a plan – make a blueprint or plan of your house or their bedroom
- Plan a trip to the city or a holiday to work out the action steps and then see how the plan is carried out
- Design a new layout of the bedroom or a room in the house
- Build or make something out of remnants, cardboard boxes, ice cream sticks etc.
- Play an instrument – experiment with sounds and singing
- Count coins or buttons and sort them to create different number patterns or equations
- Collect items from nature and categorise by colour, shape, object
- Jigsaw puzzles
- Computer coding
- Card games
- Board games
- Chess and other strategy games
- Maths quizzes
- Rock hunts
- Insect and bug hunts
- Make a "how to" video on a topic of interest to your child
- Build something mechanical using pulleys or gears
- Build a model boat
- Make paper planes and have a plane throwing competition.

Iconic visual and verbal learning at home

- Conversations to share ideas, thoughts, opinions
- Draw or paint and share ideas that appear in the artwork
- Watch a movie together and share thoughts and ideas
- Invent a new idea to solve an environmental, social or home problem

- Observe nature then create or design a collage or representation of what they see
- Use leaves and other items from nature to create an image
- Observe and discuss the colours, shapes, numbers while in the car or on a walk
- Weave fabric or paper
- Cut paper art
- Family excursions to a farm, camping, beach, zoo, etc; then ask your child to draw or describe the day verbally
- Create a board game with rules and instructions.

Symbolic/Right brain categoric learning at home

- Observe nature – identify species of plants, trees and animals
- Read and identify objects, characters and animals in the book
- Guessing games – I spy, trivia, guess what, etc
- Play with plastic animals, dinosaurs, cars and encourage grouping
- Go camping and ask children to collect items they find and group them into categories
- Collect items from nature and categorise by colour, shape, object
- Take photos and create a scrapbook of grouped items to compare and contrast – identify their similarities and differences.

These are just some of the activities you can facilitate to encourage the **cognitive skills** of:

- Creativity
- Curiosity
- Critical thinking to solve a problem or prove a theory
- Following instructions – comprehend and organise classification schemes and concepts well
- Understanding patterns or processes
- Having a good understanding of spatial relations – space between objects
- Coordination of small objects and visual details
- Comprehension and good communication of ideas and abstract thinking
- Following directions

- Communication of verbal and visual ideas
- Concentration and the ability to not become bored with repetitive actions
- Understanding meanings of words and instructions
- Understanding of maths word and visual maths problems
- Attention to detail
- Observation skills
- Visual memory for details
- Seeing connections when reading or playing games
- Fast word recognition
- Decision making
- Listening and responding
- Memorising verbal instructions and carrying out the instruction
- Memorising visual instructions and then carrying out the instruction
- Holding information in the mind and recalling or retelling
- Memorising numbers
- Memorising symbols
- Recognising numbers
- Recognising symbols
- Seeing and identifying things from different perspectives – up, down, side, below, above, before, after
- Connecting facts
- Maths and literacy vocabulary
- Ability to carry out a task or create without specific instructions
- Understanding and exploring consequences of actions
- Creative words and ideas
- Sense of humour
- Developing rapport and inter relational skills.

Non-cognitive skills being developed through a child participating in activities are:

- Developing rapport and interpersonal skills
- Ability to read and respond to another person
- Perseverance
- Learning to take turns
- Patience
- Teamwork
- Negotiating
- Learning to lose a game and try again

- Patience
- Motivation
- Openness to new experiences
- Conscientiousness
- Flexibility
- Extraversion
- Agreeableness
- Emotional regulation
- Communication
- Relationship skills
- Interpersonal skills
- Co-operation
- Optimistic attitude.

It's possible you may already be facilitating many of these learning at home activities, but perhaps you may not realise how effective these opportunities are in nurturing different styles of learning, including developing cognitive and non-cognitive skills. These are essential skills in understanding how to gather thoughts and ideas, data and information, to prompt questions and explore their relevance, analyse and develop solutions from the information provided – all skills that are needed for children to excel in literacy and numeracy at school which are the foundations for all learning throughout their formal learning and beyond.

By actively facilitating activities, you are creating opportunities for learning anytime, anywhere, enabling your child's cognitive learning skills to develop. Through practice, it will become second nature for your child to think and act in ways that develop many of the skills needed to learn at school and function in life. These are essentially the most important life skills, to be able to excel in literacy and numeracy, to think and create, to be able to problem solve and interpret information on a daily basis – we all need to do this to effectively function but it also enhances broader intellectual capabilities and academic learning in so many ways.

There is no doubt that if you have a positive attitude and are willing to work alongside teachers in partnership to assist your child, children are ultimately the beneficiaries. I encourage you to ask teachers for information on what strategies they are teaching the children so you can use consistent terminology and understand other ways to support their learning at home using the example activities I've shared with you.

When it comes to supporting reading in the early years of school, there are many skills children learn. You may ask your child questions while reading to enhance their cognitive skills in understanding what is happening in the story. Depending on what the focus is for reading and literacy at school, you can provide support at home with simple tasks like listening and asking questions, supporting your child's understanding, comprehension and thinking about the story and other types of learning from the list of skills.

It is beneficial for children to know that reading is important in all subject areas and that there are resources available in their local community to support their learning. It also shows you are interested in their learning and creating a learning environment at home. You are also able to foster a passion for reading a range of books, including audio books or graphic narratives, rather than just reading text-based books.

Here are suggestions for some questions you may ask while reading together. Once again, you don't need to ask all of these at once or you may overwhelm your child. A couple of times a week, choose two or three questions from the list to strengthen your child's reading and comprehension skills.

- What do you think the story is about?
- Who are the characters in the story?
- What are their names?
- How are they different from each other?
- What are their similarities?
- What are the messages in the story?
- What is happening in the story?
- Why is it happening?
- Why is this important?
- Why do you think the character does this?
- Why do you think that's important for the story?
- How are you similar to and different from the characters in the story?
- Which character do you identify with most?

You can ask other questions that come to mind while you are reading the story together – ask about colours, shapes, characters, pictures, symbols or objects in the story. And don't forget sometimes to just read together for fun.

There is a distinct difference between teaching as a professional and supporting your child through learning at home. The teacher has been trained specifically to teach children to learn the school curriculum. They use certain techniques, strategies and methods to do this, including methods to improve cognitive skills. As you have learned, there are numerous ways to support aspects of this learning in their social, emotional development that are also related to cognitive and non-cognitive skills.

More in-depth engagement at home involves specific targeted learning, such as supporting maths or literacy and what your child is specifically learning at school. You may need more instruction by the teacher for you to engage in learning by asking questions or providing other information for your child to be able to complete a task or project. An example might be when children are learning specific words or mathematical problems, or how to understand the content of a book. If the teacher informs you of this and what your child needs to practice or learn, you are able to focus on specific ways to support your child that will target improvement in that particular area of their learning. Another example might be if your child is learning to tell the time, you might be asked to talk about this at home and find different ways that time is presented in the home and out in the community. Or if your child is learning about syllables you might ask them to find as many words with two, three and four syllables. Once again, communication between you and the teacher is important in order to understand what sort of support you can provide at home that relates to what they are currently learning at school.

Ultimately if you focus on initiating some of the activities I listed to enhance cognitive and non-cognitive skills, there is more chance of your child as enjoying learning at school as they are able to apply these skills..

In summary, some of the many ways you can actively and intentionally engage in learning at home are:
- Provide resources and extra learning activities and opportunities linked with what your child is learning at school to enhance their understanding, comprehension and interest in what they are learning.

- Take a genuine interest in their learning and in other school activities they participate in and provide support and encouragement.
- Provide feedback when required to build confidence and support your child to persevere and improve, or to recognise and acknowledge when they have done great work.
- Understand how children learn, what their strengths are, where they need support and how you can support them at home.
- Understand their passions, interests and how to enable, encourage and nurture them.
- Seek advice from teachers about learning goals to strengthen their cognitive learning abilities through activities at home.
- Celebrate with the teacher and the child when those goals are achieved – you are a circle of support that needs to be congratulated.
- Celebrate with your child when they reach other personal learning goals at home, focusing on their strengths in supporting them to improve and learn how to manage and become more independent – they need to be praised when this happens so they know they are learning and growing, moving towards becoming an independent, confident and capable person.
- Keep track of where your child is with their progress and support them with extra help if they need it – you may need to understand the learning criteria that your child is working to achieve and understand where they are currently in their learning progress. Focus on discussing their learning growth with them and their teachers rather than just a letter or number result to determine your child's progress or success.
- Read school reports and other communication to keep up to date and to take action on recommendations from teachers – during parent-teacher conferences, ask questions about learning goals so you can understand how to support your child to reach their next goal.
- Understand what is expected of your child while at school and support them to meet these expectations.

- Develop your own confidence to seek advice and ask questions of the teacher as a valued member of the circle of support for your child.

There is plenty of literature you may like to explore on how humans learn and other parent engagement activities that develop the functions of the brain. Knowing that you have the capacity to facilitate enhanced learning at home will impact your child and their learning capacity. Always remember that your child is learning at a pace that suits them; that learning should be fun; and your child needs to know they have your support and guidance as this provides them with more opportunities to thrive.

Chapter 9

FEEDBACK FOR LEARNING IMPROVEMENT

*The most powerful single moderator that
enhances achievement, is feedback.*

PROFESSOR JOHN HATTIE (2008)

One of the most difficult roles you may have as a parent is encouraging and motivating your children to learn. One challenging task for parents can be giving feedback. Feedback can either be an opportunity for your child to understand how they are going and any areas for improvement, or it could be taken as criticism. Feedback from a teacher can be very different to feedback from a parent. There are more emotions involved when feedback comes from you, as your child will often be trying to meet your expectations. Children need feedback as they learn so they know they are on the right track. The power of feedback can impact a child and their ability to achieve and progress in their learning.

Homework is one method for parents to gauge how their child is progressing, in between reading school reports or formal meetings with teachers. Parents may use homework as an opportunity to provide feedback. However, they are not always equipped with the skills to deliver feedback in an effective and relevant way that supports the child. This can result in homework becoming a battleground and can cause tension between a parent and child. It's unfortunate that parents are often put in a position of having to police homework instead of being enabled to engage in the learning and provide appropriate and effective feedback. In my experience, there was no guidance for parents in this specific area.

As a parent, understanding your child and their capabilities, and being mindful of their sensitivities to certain types of feedback, is important to avoid conflict where possible. It's also important to understand how to give feedback that can actually make a difference. It's also helpful to be mindful of whether your feedback is necessary.

If a child is constantly praised and put on a pedestal, and is not provided with honest, timely and constructive feedback, they may not be able to cope when they are challenged. It can be tricky to know how to strike a balance between providing positive feedback to encourage the child, and providing constructive feedback in a way that is not taken personally by the child.

Your role is to help your child to challenge themselves in a way that gently encourages them to try harder according to their level of ability. Sometimes this can feel pushy, but encouragement and appropriate feedback can enhance your child's understanding of their potential, that they are capable of achieving more, or can encourage them in knowing they are on the right track.

Feedback is one of the five principles in Locke's Goal-Setting Theory, created by Edwin Locke and Gary Latham in the 1960s.

> Never allow a student to "do their best" as this is the goal with the least challenge; everything the student does can be claimed as their best!
>
> The inherent nature of learning is that there is a gap between the feedback and the attainment of goals. Feedback allows them to set reasonable goals and to track their performance in relation to their goals so that adjustments in effort, direction and even strategy can be made as needed (Sari 2018).

The other four goal setting principles are clarity, challenge, commitment and task complexity, and these are still relevant today. Children need *clarity* to understand the goals, they need to be *challenged* to reach those goals, they need to be *committed* and able to reach the goals through various levels of *complexity*.

We often say to our children, "Just do your best." This can vary from child to child and may not be beneficial in challenging children to excel beyond what they believe are their capabilities. Their understanding of their best may not actually be their best effort. Encouraging children to challenge themselves and to push just that little bit further is not going to harm them if approached in a way that benefits them as a learner in not being afraid to challenge themselves with more complex tasks. This comes back to the importance of developing their cognitive skills that build their confidence and thought processes to be able to identify and solve problems.

If your expectation for your child is that they do their best every time, when they are unaware of what their best actually is, they may be working towards goals that are unclear. It is better to discuss their learning goals first so they know what they are aiming for and so you also know where they are heading, otherwise everything they do could be seen as their best effort or they may never realise their true potential.

In 2020 I attended an Education Summit in Melbourne and listened to a presentation by local academic and teacher, Ben Lawless, on the reporting of progress for students. The method of reporting he discussed was focused on the progression of skills and the growth that occurs over time, rather than focusing on only the end result as a symbol of progress. As parents, we are often conditioned to believe results are the end goal, without knowing the extent of growth and progress achieved by our children over time – this demonstrates to children that the end result is all that matters.

Some people may only praise children for success if they achieve a high score or mark. If parents are not made aware of their child's achievements along the way, praising a child only once they achieve the result can somewhat diminish the impact of the end result for the child. One of the confusing aspects of knowing how your child is progressing is understanding what actually constitutes a high mark and what it takes for a child to achieve it. Much of the reporting of learning is a summary or snapshot rather than a detailed account of progress and you may be none the wiser about any gaps in your child's learning or how this could be improved, unless you enquire about this with teachers. Parent and teacher meetings are a good opportunity for you to ask questions about what skills, qualities, attitudes, achievements and growth helped them to achieve the result, and to ask teachers to further explain academic reports if you don't understand how your child achieved their results.

In some cases children may feel as though their learning results are not for them but to please others or to reach the appropriate standards set by others. What we really need to focus on is the child's understanding of their own progress and achievements along the way, for them to take ownership of their learning as they go, rather than just focusing on the end result. While this is the bonus at the finish line, it is a fleeting moment in time. The progression and improvement of skills learned is actually more important and rewarding in the long run.

In the keynote address at the education conference, my interpretation of what Lawless shared is that children who are high achievers or top performers are not necessarily the best learners, nor do they progress very far – they are often good keepers of knowledge, as they are able to memorise and relay information, but understanding and applying what they've actually learned may not be exposed in the final result unless they are tested with more complex problems to solve. They may be missing other necessary cognitive skills to be able to think more creatively and critically, to be flexible in their thinking and practical in their application of ideas.

Reflecting on the vision you have created (or are yet to create) for your child's education and what your expectations are for them, consider reflecting on ways you can support them through the process and progress of their learning, rather than only focusing on achieving high results. This will allow you to frame how you provide feedback on your child's progress and to have an understanding that learning is a process that takes time. The end result is actually the product of the learning itself. The essential skills children learn and achieve are what matters most of all.

When your child asks for your opinion on their grades or results, it would be helpful to know what the specific learning intention was to begin with, and then to ask for their opinion on how they would rate their learning efforts before providing your answer. This helps them to self assess what they are aiming to achieve in the first place, whether or not they feel they are progressing, and if they could do better or need further support. Self assessment is a form of feedback and builds a child's confidence as an independent learner.

When my children approached me for feedback, I often found myself saying to them, "I believe you can do better," then regretting it and feeling bad for being too pushy and making it about me and my opinion. Perhaps I could have rephrased my response to, "How did you think you went?" or "Do you think you could improve in this area?" or "Do you need support to improve in the areas you're not sure about?" These questions give ownership of learning to your child and encourage them to think about their own progress rather than focusing on your opinion or pleasing you. However, you can also use questions like these to gauge if your child actually understands their progress and if they do need support. Your role as their guide is to gently encourage them to improve and test themselves to see what they are genuinely capable of achieving.

One of the ways schools provide guidance for student progress is with the use of rubrics, learning intentions or criteria for students to follow and aim for. This means students are able to see what the learning expectations are along the way, to have the clarity they need to take steps required to achieve the end result. Therefore, instead of highlighting mistakes and what they've done wrong, there is more focus on what is required of them to achieve at various levels of competency.

The feedback you provide has an influence on how your children view themselves as learners. Feedback can have an impact on a child's self-esteem and their motivation to learn or even to attend school. When it comes to providing feedback and encouragement as a parent, particularly when it comes to children's academic learning, it can be tricky if you don't have the information you need, such as a learning rubric or criteria, to make a constructive judgement. You may ask your child to show you their learning rubric as a way of understanding the level they are at and what they are aiming to achieve. When you are on the same page as the teacher and your child, it makes it easier for you to engage and provide relevant feedback if requested by your child or by their teacher.

Using these measurement tools allows students to self assess which level they are aiming for and enables them to determine if and where they need further support to reach a certain milestone or level in their learning. They may consult with the teacher about this and you may also discuss this with teachers as a point of reference in how your child is progressing and to understand any areas for improvement. These are actually more helpful in many ways than school reports as they specifically state the learning expectations and skills needed to reach a certain level of learning ability.

Your expectations of your child may be completely different to that of the school. This is when conflicts can arise, especially if the learning process has not been explained to parents. This can occur through your own interpretation of what is required or maybe how you were taught at school. This is why it is so important to understand the learning process and criteria and the types of feedback that teachers use at school that you can also adopt to support your child at home.

I recall that while reading my children's school reports there was a gap in my understanding of how my children had achieved their final results. I wasn't always sure of what they were learning at specific times; I wasn't understanding the context of their learning or what goals they were trying to reach. In some cases, when trying to support them with homework, the children themselves were not always sure of what they were trying to achieve. It is challenging to be on the same page with your children when trying to provide support, encouragement and feedback with little or no knowledge of what the context, purpose or outcome is supposed to be.

Feedback needs to be directed at the different stages that children are currently with their learning. I recall when my children sought feedback on their homework in primary school. Not realising the learning was focussed on specific stages of learning at the time, I proceeded to correct spelling but was told by my child that spelling wasn't the focus of the homework. Instead I was to give feedback on grammar and punctuation. I looked at this in two different ways. My first reaction was that I believe spelling is also important to correct. Then I recognised that this was how my child was being taught to understand their learning and take ownership of specific areas of focus. It was simply that this information had not been communicated to parents to enable the delivery of appropriate and contextual feedback related to learning goals.

At times I would look at their homework and feel helpless, wondering what sort of feedback I could or should provide them, or if I needed to just leave that to the teacher. It was at these times that I questioned what my role was and whether the feedback I was providing was effective or if it was negatively impacting my child. With no guidance, I felt out of my depth and, like most parents in this position, ready to give up.

One of the strategies Professor John Hattie and Helen Timperley (2017) suggest for teachers that can also be used by parents at home is corrective feedback, which is effective for certain subjects, such as mathematics and spelling where there are correct and incorrect answers to specific questions or problems.

This position of the "corrector" didn't always sit well with me, as I felt this type of feedback was somewhat authoritarian and wasn't always received well by my children. I wasn't even sure it was my role to correct their mistakes. Instead, I tried asking a question about a word to see if my child had seen the word before and if they knew how to spell it. We often read books in our home and this helped enormously with many cognitive skills including comprehension, spelling and recognising letters, symbols, words and story concepts. I found that when giving feedback, asking the children questions to provide opportunities for them to find the answers was more effective in helping them recognise when a word was spelled incorrectly.

Some positive questions you can ask to encourage your child to find the answers include

- "Does that word look right to you?"
- "Do you think that is spelled correctly?"
- "Where do you think you may have seen that word before?"
- "How can you say the word by sounding the letters and does it sound right?"

There are other spelling strategies that children learn at school, so speak with the teacher about them so you can ask your child appropriate questions as a way of giving corrective feedback. You can encourage your child to use the strategies they are learning at school without feeling like you need to give them the answer as part of the feedback, no matter how tempted you are to do so. Your feedback depends on their age group, what the homework involves, what the learning expectations are and what sort of feedback they need.

Sometimes you might be faced with unusual questions or situations that require common sense to provide constructive feedback. When I provide feedback to my child, I'm conscious of whether it is positive or negative and how it may be interpreted or received. The results of effective feedback, according to a research review by Hattie and Timperley, "can increase the likelihood that students will return to or persist in an activity and self report higher interest in the activity" (2007).

Children will respond to feedback differently or may never seek your feedback about their learning. Some of the key points raised by Hattie and Timperley about the effectiveness of feedback on students include:

- The level of self efficacy (a belief in their learning capacity, motivation, behaviour and ability to reach their goals) of the student by the student affects how they receive feedback.

- Sometimes less feedback is more effective to encourage more problem solving and working out how to get out of being 'stuck'.
- Encouraging children to ask questions to become 'unstuck', such as "where am I now, where am I going, where to next, how can I improve?"
- Seeking feedback from your child is effective because it means they share their learning with you which then reinforces areas they may need support.
- Knowing when to give feedback. If your child is struggling or feeling frustrated, allowing them to take a break and come back to the task. During the break they may actually discover the answers they are seeking or still need your feedback.

Hattie and Timperley (2017) describe other forms of feedback that are less effective:

- Punishment
- Extrinsic and intrinsic rewards
- Immediate vs delayed

Punishment

Punishment may be a method given to children as a consequence when they don't meet parents' or school's expectations. This is not a productive or effective method for encouraging or supporting children and their learning, even though it was a method used by schools and parents in the past. Listening to children and giving them a voice to express where they feel they are challenged, and working together on ways to improve, are more appropriate and effective responses than punishing them.

Speaking negatively about a child is a form of punishment. Some children are punished in other ways for not doing well at school. Children shouldn't be punished for below-standard achievement. It is likely they need more support, they may learn in different ways, or they may be struggling socially and/or emotionally. These and other environmental factors can have a huge impact on children's ability to concentrate and complete tasks effectively. Punishment does nothing to support a child. To be listened to and understood, however, will have a more positive impact on their confidence, self esteem, ability and motivation to learn.

If, when children receive feedback, they react defensively or they want to quit, or if you threaten punishment for lack of achievement, they may develop a closed mindset and their confidence and self esteem may be impacted.

Confidence doesn't only come from positive feedback. It also comes from the knowledge that receiving constructive feedback and making mistakes is a normal part of learning. Children need to learn there is always a solution and ways to improve if they make mistakes. Your role in giving feedback is to encourage them to explore ways of solving problems. It is then they are able to grow in confidence.

If your child is struggling, and you give in and do the work for them, they will become reliant on you to solve their problems for them. This in itself is a form of feedback, showing them that they can give up if it gets too difficult and rely on others to fix the problem. This isn't serving them well for future learning and life challenges. If they refuse to cooperate you can suggest taking a break and coming back to it later rather than doing it for them or punishing them.

Coaching questions are much more effective in providing feedback because they aren't correcting or judging, but offering the child the opportunity to self-reflect, self-correct and realise that they have control over their learning as well as your support. You are showing an interest by asking questions and you are not passing judgement on their performance. Rather, you are encouraging them to self-assess and self-manage, to find the answers themselves. Self-awareness and mindfulness in providing feedback is so important in developing their growth mindset.

If you can see that your child is having difficulty understanding a task, you can work out other ways to help them understand the concepts. Don't be afraid to be creative or to draw on your own experiences. Tell stories, use analogies or show them other examples to help them understand. We can sometimes forget that learning should be fun. It can provide opportunities for you to build a connection with your child, to explore the answers together or to experiment and laugh at yourselves when you make mistakes.

Learning isn't about getting it right and being perfect every time. If you view making mistakes or failing as a bad thing, your children will too. If they are criticised or punished for making mistakes or not doing well, they may be afraid of making mistakes for fear of either punishment or failure. This may then impact their motivation for learning, causing blockages or 'stuckness', and prevent them from trying in the first place.

Extrinsic and intrinsic rewards

Motivation for learning can be connected to extrinsic (external) rewards or intrinsic (internal) rewards.

Extrinsic rewards are tangible rewards such as:
- Trophies, ribbons, other prizes
- Monetary rewards
- Prizes.

Intrinsic rewards are internal feelings or experiences such as:
- Pride in your work
- Feelings of respect, acknowledgement or validation from others
- Personal growth
- Fulfilment of a purpose
- Doing work that's enjoyable
- Feelings of accomplishment.

When it comes to prizes or monetary rewards as a method of appraisal or feedback, there are pros and cons to consider. I was recently involved in a conversation between some parents who were discussing their children's progress at school. One child had done particularly well and was receiving a reward for her efforts. The other child being discussed had not done so well at school and was being criticised for the lack of effort and achievement. In the past the child had been doing really well at school and comments such as, "I don't know what's wrong with her," and, "It's not like her," demonstrated a disconnect or lack of understanding of the child and what she may have been struggling with and where she needed support.

Viewing lack of achievement as a problem demonstrates a lack of understanding of where improvements are needed to support the child. Much of this stems from our perceptions of education being about high achievement rather than a gradual progression or a process as discussed earlier. We have been conditioned to think this way from when we ourselves were students – I remember a definite divide between the high achievers who were always rewarded, the students who hovered in the middle, and those who were "failing". I see many schools today still glorifying the high achievers but not the other students – who may have put in massive efforts and grown as learners and as people, but who haven't achieved the end result that is viewed as the pinnacle. Progressive achievements should be recognised as valuable in the learning process and acknowledged as part of formal education.

Often when listening to parent conversations, there is sometimes a tone of competitiveness, a form of one-upmanship that "my child is better than yours". There are often comparisons between children and siblings in these conversations. While there is nothing wrong with being proud of your child and what they are achieving, they need to hear and know of your pride more than the rest of the world. I am more conscious now of when and how I discuss my children and their achievements, particularly if they are in the room. We sometimes forget they are listening and in some cases seeing what may be posted online about them. This is also a type of feedback that can affect both their self-esteem and their relationship with you.

Rewards are a method used by some parents to encourage their children to do well at school. You may believe that offering monetary rewards or presents will mean they will rise to the challenge. However, if you offer rewards, would they be meeting that challenge for their own academic achievement, to achieve the short-term reward, or to satisfy parent expectations? Consider whether this encourages self motivation to achieve their own goals and whether this is the best form of motivation for them.

In life, we don't always receive physical or financial rewards for our efforts, nor do we always receive recognition. Intrinsic rewards are a sense of satisfaction that you have set yourself a goal and achieved it. The process and progress along the way are ultimately what will contribute to happiness and a sense of achievement. Whilst receiving a reward or an award can be an extra special element in reaching our potential, so too is being humble in our achievements. Motivation by award or reward alone isn't sustainable and can potentially lead to developing a sense of entitlement to a reward each time you achieve a goal. It's a tough life lesson when this isn't forthcoming.

Awards are sometimes given to children at school. Many schools provide awards as recognition for student academic achievement, such as "student of the week" awards. Other schools provide awards for good citizenship, good behaviour and sport achievements. In some schools they present awards to each student for participation to encourage further engagement. There is a fine balance between offering an incentive to win an award versus being offered a reward for achievement. Ultimately it is up to parents to decide, however I would encourage you to think about the outcome of introducing extrinsic rewards to children as a way to motivate them to do well at school.

In life, everyone is good at something, but not everyone is or can be good at everything. Even if you come sixth or seventh in a race, it doesn't mean you have failed. It may mean you could improve or strengthen your skills, practice more, try harder next time or try something else. We need to encourage children to change their perception of losing or not quite meeting the expectations of others or themselves. Coming second can be a positive and a motivation to keep persevering to come first. With further training, effort and strength or perseverance, the result might improve... but it might not and that's ok. I recently had a discussion with my son about how I was always in the B-team in netball at school; it took me years to reach the A-team. He was feeling despondent about constantly being picked in the B-team and was talking negatively about himself. I shared my own experience with him to demonstrate that if you are determined enough to reach the goal of being picked in the A-team, you need to work out a plan to reach that goal, be clear on where you want to go, have the commitment to stick to the plan and take action to eventually get to where you want to be. You may have some stories like this you can share with your children to let them know to continue to persevere. This in itself is good feedback when your child starts to give up. Sharing stories is a great strategy as it makes them see that it is possible to keep trying and to eventually achieve what they want.

Children need to be encouraged to embrace every experience as an opportunity to learn, to persevere or try something new. Many people who have lost or failed have gone on to achieve great things because they never gave up.

Immediate vs delayed feedback

Immediate feedback has the capability of rewarding the nervous system with a hit of dopamine, making it more motivating than delayed feedback.

I witnessed an example of immediate feedback used by one of my children's teachers, who explained methods used in her maths class. The children completed three maths equations and then had to line up at her desk for immediate feedback on whether they were on the right track or not. The children were then provided with an explanation of where they needed to improve and were given three more equations to complete and line up again. Chunking down tasks and giving feedback was the strategy adopted, which you can also use at home when your child is asked to complete a task either by you or for homework. Set two or three smaller and shorter tasks then give immediate feedback, then give them three more.

The teacher found this strategy more effective than making the students do the whole sheet of equations before receiving delayed feedback at the end of class or the next day – when they've potentially forgotten what they learned. Immediate feedback provided them with the confidence that they were able to complete the tasks, understand and remember what they had learned and feel confident to complete the work correctly next time.

When it comes to children's behaviour it is also important to use immediate feedback where possible to demonstrate where they can improve.

According to Hattie and Timperley (2007), effective feedback should answer these three questions:

1. Where am I going? (What are my goals?)
2. How am I going? (What progress is being made towards reaching the goals?)
3. Where to next? (What activities need to be undertaken to make better progress?)

You can use these questions if your child is seeking feedback to help coach them to find the answers or so you can both find a solution. If you are unsure of how and when to provide feedback you can use the strategies suggested and I also encourage you to:

- Ask the teacher or learning leader what the children are learning at school – what they are specifically focussing on as part of their learning process and how you can provide effective and relevant feedback for your child that is going to encourage and help them improve.
- Develop a positive partnership with your child's teacher to enable you to understand the goals or criteria for the learning progress expectations. You want to aim to receive from the teacher appropriate information and skills to be able to provide feedback for your child.

- Provide feedback only when necessary. You can support and reinforce what the teacher is trying to achieve at school but only if you have received this information.
- Try to avoid material rewards, as they set up the child for future expectations. Explore other ways to motivate your child to learn by engaging in conversation, exploring their feelings to access these through their learning, understanding and supporting their interests and increasing your knowledge of their learning style by observing them and how they learn. If you are unsure of what to look for, speak with their teacher about this.
- Provide positive and constructive feedback by asking questions and making suggestions like, "Perhaps you could try it this way," or, "Have you tried the strategy you learned at school?" or other questions that are appropriate for the situation.
- Be aware of your tone of voice when providing feedback. We learned earlier about the various learning styles and how they impact an individual and their ability to learn. Auditory people are particularly sensitive to tone of voice and this can affect the type of feedback you are providing. Using a calm tone of voice and building rapport, means your child is more likely to respond calmly and be more willing to listen to what you are saying. Choose your words carefully and keep the focus on your child and their learning potential.
- Talk with your child about what sort of feedback they prefer.

Motivation to learn

There may come a time during your child's education where they lack the motivation to learn or to attend school. This is a tricky space to navigate but there are some ways that you can help your child overcome these challenges and support them to be more self-motivated.

When we learn, we experience feelings, and these are extremely important to focus on. The feelings associated with learning that parents shared in Chapter 8 (euphoria, empowerment, persistence, arousing curiosity) are all connected to a natural reward in the body's nervous system – dopamine. Dopamine is a chemical released in the brain that makes you feel good. It helps nerve cells to send messages to each other and, according to professor of neurobiology and ophthalmology at Stanford

School of Medicine, Dr Andrew Huberman, any system that taps into the dopamine system is also connected with neuroplasticity.

When you are learning or trying to achieve a goal, experiencing those good feelings makes learning and taking action more enjoyable. This is a coaching technique and many salespeople also use it to almost trick the brain into having a good feeling by focusing on the end goal as the reward and attaching your thoughts to that end goal. For example, if there is a task that needs to be completed that you may find boring, such as cleaning the house or doing dishes, instead of focusing on the task, you can train your brain to focus on the end intrinsic reward of *how you will feel* once it the task is completed – that feeling you get when the house is clean; feeling more in control, having a clearer mind – to feel good and proud of yourself. This is a motivating tool you can use to get the job done. The reward is the good feeling that comes from the body releasing dopamine. The physical outcome is an added bonus.

Another way to trick the brain is to focus on the shadow values discussed in Chapter 6: seeking attention, authority, belonging, control, rebellion, superiority, validation.

Use the feelings you receive from having your shadow values met to achieve the dopamine hit. Using shadow values in this way is a technique I use in coaching and on myself as a motivational tool to help clients overcome barriers to them taking action.

> Test this out on yourself first and then you can use it to motivate your child if they are struggling to complete a task.
>
> Think of one of the shadow values, such as rebellion.
>
> Think of a time when you have rebelled and focus on the feeling of rebellion.
>
> How does it feel when you rebel?
>
> You may feel a sense of control, self belief and satisfaction that you are going against the grain. It is very easy for the brain to access the feeling of rebellion and use it to rebel against any negative thoughts that are telling you not to take action.

For example, if I'm trying to lose weight and I am tempted by certain foods, I can tell my brain to rebel against those thoughts and remind myself that if I eat those foods I'm not going to achieve my goal. I can rebel against my own desire to eat something I know is not going to get me what I want. The idea is to train your brain to receive a dopamine rush from achieving your end goal rather than eating the wrong foods and then feeling bad about yourself. Accessing the dopamine through the feeling of rebellion and achievement is very powerful. Of course, it takes practice and discipline to do this but this technique can be very effective.

When children are learning, if they are unmotivated or uninspired by the learning, you can help them to access the feelings that different shadow values give them. If they don't like a particular topic at school – such as history for example – think of a way that you can tap into the feelings they get from topics they do like – such as art. You may help them see that history is connected to art, ask them to draw what they are learning in history, or suggest they visualise it. Once they achieve a similar "good feeling" they will receive a natural hit of dopamine that then motivates them to want to learn more. Seeing the connection between what they are learning and how they are feeling provides them with a reason to engage in history.

Using the shadow value of control as an example, you could ask your child to take control of their learning. If they are feeling lazy or complaining about the work, help them to take control of those thoughts and not let negative thoughts beat them or prevent them from achieving their learning goal. You can ask them to create a character in their imagination that represents the "naysayer" in their mind that's telling them they can't do it. Once they have that character in their mind, they can talk with the character and take control of their thoughts. This might sound strange but it's a very powerful coaching tool to help manage thoughts and take back control. If your child values control they can access that feeling by not giving in to the negative thoughts that prevent them from taking action.

Another way to help children with motivation is to focus on one small task at a time. This is a coaching technique called "chunking". If the process to reach the end goal seems monumental, chunking can help break tasks down into smaller, achievable steps. One small step at a time turns into two small steps, three, four and so on until the end goal is reached. The body achieves a natural dopamine hit at every step along the way and the learning process itself becomes the reward.

Ultimately, providing feedback is just one strategy that can be used to support your child with their learning at home. If delivered effectively, in a way that is encouraging and helps to improve your child's progress, it can make a huge difference for your child and their motivation to learn. Even more effective is when you are working in partnership and on the same page with the teacher so you are able to give appropriate and relevant feedback to suit your child's learning abilities and goals. When children know they are supported and they value your feedback, it's another way of improving your child's learning.

Chapter 10
SUPPORTING AN ENTREPRENEURIAL MINDSET

> Your time is limited, so don't waste it living someone else's life. Don't be trapped by dogma – which is living with the results of other people's thinking. Don't let the noise of other's opinions drown out your own inner voice. And most important, have the courage to follow your heart and intuition. They somehow already know what you truly want to become. Everything else is secondary.
>
> STEVE JOBS (2005)

Life, we are told, is about aspiring to be something or someone, to make a difference or to build a legacy, to live each day with intention and to grow as a person. Humans can aspire to be and do what they wish to, what they imagine and what they dream about. However, there are many aspects of life that can hinder or prevent people from fully exploring their true potential. It is not a journey you can take alone. The support of others is needed to achieve dreams but the choice of who you want to be and what you want to do with your life is yours and yours alone.

You can encourage your children to dream and design the life they aspire to have. To do this you will need to learn to guide, rather than control, to observe rather than ignore or dismiss, to trust that when you intentionally focus on creating strong foundations for them, they are able to grow in confidence to make the choices for their life that they are being called to make. Children trust you to guide them. They look to you for the light that guides the way. Your own light may have dimmed because you've forgotten what it's like to be wide eyed, curious, eager to learn, explore, ask questions, take risks and discover the answers. Such enthusiasm and curiosity is a gift that many children have and bring to our worlds. They remind us of what's possible through imagination and their unique views and perspectives.

When children are young they often share the most profound statements or dreams. These can sometimes be dismissed as not possible, but it's during these early years that they need to be encouraged to follow those dreams, that thought or idea, that profound knowledge they seem to have at such a young age.

In 2022 at the National Catholic Education Conference in Melbourne, I was lucky enough to see and learn from keynote speaker Dr Jordan Nguyen, a biomedical engineer, author, TV presenter and technology futurist. In his presentation he shared how he encourages students, educators and parents to dare to dream big and explore the possibilities of creativity and critical thinking to understand the human brain and make a difference for people.

Nguyen shared how the power of the mind combined with technology can provide opportunities for humanity never thought possible before. He shared some of the stories of paraplegics and those with cerebral palsy he has worked with who are now able to enjoy the wonders of movement again, through inventions that adopt various technologies such as "artificial intelligence, virtual reality, new techniques in 3D human scanning, neuroscience, and the ideas of human consciousness."

His inventions have enabled paraplegics to experience a wheelchair that can be controlled by the mind and eyes. This provides independence for those who are reliant on others to move them around, improving their sense of wellbeing and purpose.

Other inventions that use the power of the mind and technology have enabled disabled people to play music, drive a car, and be virtually transported to other countries they may not be able to visit physically. Nguyen explains artificial intelligence as simply the "ability to figure out the difference between us and our environment and us and other people". He shared that a robot is only as clever and inhibited as we are as intelligent beings. Jordan's inventions explore opportunities to use that intelligence for good, through robotics, virtual reality, the power of electricity or energy in the body, eye movement and other forms of technology. Another invention is enabling parents to see the cognitive abilities their disabled children have through eye tracking technology, essentially providing the child who is unable to express themselves verbally with a different way to communicate.

If something doesn't exist yet, it doesn't mean it can't be invented. The limitations of our minds and any fears that we have perceived can prevent the creation of new solutions to the issues and challenges of humanity. Nguyen shared during the presentation that children are technological natives and need to be encouraged to find ways to use technology to change the lives of others in appropriate and positive ways.

> Be alone, that is the secret of invention;
> be alone, that is when ideas are born.
>
> NIKOLA TESLA (1934)

There are many hundreds of thousands of examples of people who have invented products and solutions to help others or advance humanity. Utilising their intelligence and ability to see what's possible has enabled many inventors, often unknown to the general public, to create useful products and services. One attribute that can contribute to creativity and can help us tune into intuition is solitude. Spending time alone and in quiet contemplation can help us listen to the ideas that may come. Being bored is a good thing because it encourages creativity. If we were bored as kids, we would create games and find things to do. When children become bored they can be restless and irritable. However, if you leave them alone and allow them time, they can find ways to fill the void and maybe even create a new idea. If my children were ever bored I would make a few suggestions but ultimately they would work out what they felt like doing. I would find them either building, designing, reading, listening to music or working on a project.

Creative and critical thinking are two essential skills required for developing the systems, products, services and other solutions to solve problems that we as a human race are facing. As we've explored through the book, these should be nurtured throughout children's education, through formal and informal learning. Creativity provides us with a way to connect with ourselves and to learn to listen to our inner voice. To allow exploring, experimenting and seeking answers. To be curious, to make connections and to discover new ways to improve our lives. It is while being creative that we are able to be in touch with our true selves, our intuitive nature that provides us with the answers we seek. This means quieting the mind and sometimes, as Tesla suggested, being alone in solitude.

Creativity allows us to view life and situations from many different perspectives and in doing so to develop empathy for others and find solutions to the complex issues that we, as a species, have often created. The ability to think allows us to make intelligent choices and decisions, providing the ability and desire to keep on learning throughout our lives. The most powerful concept that the ability to think provides for us is choice. Choices we make in our life impact our ability to achieve freedom and happiness and to enjoy the life we want to live.

The development of aspirations comes from adults enabling children's creativity and imagination to flourish, encouraging them to dream big. Children are uninhibited when they are young and have so many amazing ideas. Their perspectives and observations are quite different to adults' because they are not yet conditioned and don't necessarily attach logic or past experiences to many of the things they do. They are still asking why and how, multiple times a day. This ability to see things differently, to want to understand and learn, is so important to encourage, especially if your child shares their ideas, creations and dreams with you.

I have observed children being naturally entrepreneurial in their play as they organise each other, develop ideas for games and reveal an amazing capacity to design solutions. There is no doubt the jobs of the future will be formed by people who are creative or who have an entrepreneurial mindset and the ability to develop ideas and turn them into profitable businesses. We are seeing this taught in schools with many project-based learning activities, group collaboration on ideas and inventions, as well as the opportunity to explore and experiment through STEAM learning – Science, Technology, Engineering, Art/Design and Maths. Many children are very engaged in this type of learning as their non-cognitive and cognitive skills are strengthened, enabling them to be critical thinkers, creative and self-led learners.

I am really pleased that my own children were able to learn so many new ways to develop ideas and to bring them to life through the opportunities provided through their education and project-based learning. We were also invited to engage in these projects at home. Some of the skills the children learned included exploring concepts and developing an awareness of how to think creatively and critically, using a process and presenting a solution.

Through their inquiry unit at school, my children had the opportunity to create, use their imaginations, make an object and learn how to plan, design, make and evaluate their inventions. They were encouraged to work in teams, respond to design briefs, use mind maps, sketches, plans, diagrams and flow charts to identify situations and develop solutions to challenges. They were also asked to give and respond to feedback from their peers, and consider improvements to their project along the way, then to present their ideas to other parents and teachers.

"Entrepreneur" has become quite a buzz-word as we begin to recognise the importance of being multi-skilled, creative and critical thinkers. In her article "Creative Smarts, the Key to Career Success" (2014), Katie Cincotta explores the skills required for future employees when referring to Adobe and their findings in a global education study. The study draws a strong correlation between employability and creativity. In the article, Peter McAlpine, senior director of education for Adobe Asia Pacific states, "Creativity fosters the advanced critical thinking required of the emerging 'creative and knowledge' economies, where 'smart jobs are replacing muscle work … In this connected world, you need collaboration, you need communication and creativity and if you can get all three of those in someone, that's gold." Awareness of the skills required for future employability will provide you with opportunities to explore these with your children.

In 2012, I had the opportunity to be on a panel discussion with leading advocate of entrepreneurship, Professor Yong Zhao in Melbourne, Australia. Professor Zhao had been travelling the world to help educators understand that the future will be more reliant on creative entrepreneurs for new employment opportunities as the jobs of the past either disappear or are taken over by artificial intelligence and digital technology. Professor Zhao was well ahead of his time with his knowledge and understanding of new technologies, and was spreading the word throughout the world. In his book, *World Class Learners* (2012), Zhao suggests that there is not enough thinking in education about the impact of new technology and changes to employment opportunities. He shared that, "if there are no entrepreneurs, we need to make some. And to make some is to instil the entrepreneurship spirit into our children from the outside through education."

Zhao adds:

> It is not enough to add entrepreneurship on the perimeter – it needs to be at the core of the way education operates. Educational institutions at all levels (primary, secondary and higher education) need to adopt 21st century methods and tools to develop the appropriate learning environment for encouraging creativity, innovation and the ability to think 'out of the box' to solve problems.

Educational institutions have been gradually changing, as has the curriculum, particularly in Australia, to include general capabilities such as personal and social capability, ethical understanding, creative and critical thinking, information and communication technology and intercultural understanding.

Children are seeing and being influenced by young entrepreneurs online as the internet has made it easier to market products and services and outsource employees around the globe. Social media opened up opportunities for startups to be created and for young entrepreneurs to build online businesses, creating and selling new products and services. We've witnessed a new wave of "personal brand" influencers, many of whom are making a fortune representing other brands. Many young entrepreneurs have designed their businesses to support those in need or those who are disadvantaged.

One example is Hart Main, from Ohio, USA. At the age of thirteen, after teasing his sister about the girly scented candles she was selling for a school fundraiser, Main came up with the idea of making manly scented candles. His candle business took off and they are now handmade by the Beaver Creek Candle Company in Lisbon, Ohio, by a developmentally disabled workforce. Main invested some of his own money into the business to get it started and his parents contributed financially and supported his venture. It became a family business and they were able to work together to make it a success. "As of 2016, Main's candles are sold in every state of America, with sales exceeding six figures annually. Giving back to the community, he donates part of each sale to soup kitchens in Ohio, Pennsylvania, West Virginia, and Michigan" (Lodge 2022).

This leads me to explore how ideas start and why it's so important to encourage your children's ideas. A simple conversation between siblings and their parents who saw an opportunity meant that an idea could become a reality for Hart Main. The outcome was a thriving business but also the opportunity to give back to the community and help others. If his idea had been dismissed by his parents and others, he may not be the entrepreneur he is today and he may not have been able to help the people who have benefited from his generosity.

Another example was a young man from St Louis, Michael "Mikey" Wren who, at the tender age of eight, started Mikey's Munchies Vending, a collection of vending machines. That was just the beginning. Wren believed in helping the community by volunteering his time to teach financial literacy and hosts an annual drive to donate new toys to local kids. He has also written two children's books, *Mikey Learns About Business*, which covers writing a business plan, marketing strategies, and networking, and *Biz Is a Whiz* for children pre-K to 3. He regularly books speaking engagements to talk about his work (Lodge 2022).

There are many children who are not afraid of creating ideas and taking action. They are digital natives and use technology to their advantage, as we have seen with the emergence of video-based platforms. These young people and many more are developing ideas and, instead of just talking about it, they're taking action.

With the right attitude and the support of open-minded parents and others, children's ideas can develop. These children demonstrated qualities required to be an entrepreneur: courage, persistence, a will and drive to succeed, parental support and encouragement, and creative and critical thinking.

How to encourage creative and critical thinking

> My mother said to me,
> "If you are a soldier, you will become a general.
> If you are a monk, you will become the pope."
> Instead I was a painter and I became Picasso.
>
> PABLO PICASSO

To nurture an entrepreneurial mindset, you can use some of the strategies I shared in Chapter 8 by fostering critical and creative thinking in the home. You can expand on those examples by asking children questions and encouraging them to find the answers, then questioning them again on why or how they came up with the answer.

Encourage children to think beyond the obvious, to create more than one draft and to make mistakes and learn from them. Help them to self assess so they understand their abilities and their limitations, so they become self-motivated and self-led learners. When your child comes to you with an idea, help to nurture their thinking rather than dismissing it. The idea may not go anywhere, but keep challenging them to think about it and to improve on it, to explore other possibilities and to keep on developing ideas.

Some questions you may ask are:

- How did you come up with that idea? What was your inspiration?
- What problem is it solving?
- How does it solve the problem?
- Why is it important? (ask them this several times so they dig deeper into the idea and the purpose of the idea)
- Have you thought about …?
- How would it work practically in everyday life?
- What else can you explore to find a solution?

Encouraging perspective taking means asking them to put themselves in others' shoes. You can do this by asking them how they would feel if a situation or an event happened to them.

- How would you handle it?
- How would you react?
- What would you do?
- How would you solve the problem?

Encourage your child to use precise or specific explanations, rather than generalising or making assumptions. If they don't know the answer or need to find an answer, encourage them to research the topic and then come back to you with an explanation.

So, why aren't there more entrepreneurs around the world and why does Professor Yong Zhao believe we need to create them?

Self belief is a critical factor in following your own path, in going in a different direction to others and having the courage to make things happen. Certain influences around children can prevent them from dreaming big and seeking ways to explore ideas. It is often the desire for certainty – one of the six core human needs – that causes us as parents to guide our children towards a safe and secure job rather than taking a risk on starting a business from scratch. Uncertainty can be caused by fears you may have for your children – fear of failure, fear of not being safe, fear of not being in a secure job. Being mindful of fears and how they can hinder children's growth is critical so you can avoid projecting your fears onto them. Fears can prevent their progress and their self belief that they can achieve what they want to in life.

> **The job of an entrepreneur is not to do the job,
> it's to be the creator of jobs.**
> MIKE MICHALOWICZ, 2020

Because entrepreneurs are the creators of ideas and of jobs, there are many different skills required to manage in this role. There are now university and online training courses to teach people how to be an entrepreneur. To develop mindsets in children about the possibilities of entrepreneurship means being mindful of the way we talk with them about their future. We can encourage a new perspective from a young age and throughout their education. Encourage them to become the leaders of innovation in the future, rather than just the users or consumers of innovative ideas. While not everyone is destined to be an entrepreneur, innovation is the foundation to create change and improve how we live, how we care for each other and how we protect the planet.

In the past we've been conditioned to work hard, and yes it does take a focused, committed approach to work to achieve goals. However, with the support of technology and automation, there are now opportunities that enable people to work smarter, not harder. Only recently I heard my father telling his grandchildren that you have to "work hard to make money and things don't come easy". That may be true for some, perhaps for his generation, however this can be programmed in children as a fixed state of mind. He planted this seed in my and my siblings' minds as children and is now trying to do the same to our children. I have tried to rebel against this for years and have had to work on my mindset when it comes to how much time I spend working, my attitude to money and work/life balance. The idea that work is hard is not something I want to pass onto my children but it takes time and a different outlook to move beyond this mindset. Instead, we should encourage our children to work in jobs that fulfill them and align with their values so work doesn't become a chore, but is an enjoyable and rewarding process.

While making and having money is only one part of our lives, the seeds we plant in the minds of our children matter. Are statements like, "You must go to university to make it in this life" really true? University education enhances your knowledge and expertise and provides some options, however many successful people in business have never been to university. Some have had major learning challenges at school and have managed to build thriving businesses. Many have had to overcome the biases within their own families and education, often being told by teachers and parents they would never make it.

It takes grit and determination to make dreams come true. You have the opportunity to be mindful of the seeds you are planting in the minds of your children when it comes to their ambitions and aspirations. Providing sound advice and encouraging them to think strategically will support them in making good decisions about their future.

Two of my children had some fantastic ideas when they were young that I encouraged them to follow. One was to design clothes to fill a niche that was missing in the market for children aged ten to thirteen, an age group category commonly known as tweens. My daughter felt frustrated that she couldn't find clothes that suited that age group. They were either too young or too old for her. So I encouraged her to design some, and her ideas were amazing. I discussed with her the possibility of starting her own label. She thought about it for a while but decided that wasn't her path. She did know through this experience that I appreciated her ideas and would support her with whatever she chose as her future career. My other daughter also had some great ideas. At the age of ten she wanted to write a children's book for children who were starting school. She hired me to design the illustrations and she wrote the story. We then designed the book together and had it printed. She was able to see her idea come to life. It has now led her to become a graphic designer. The seed had been planted and she now has opportunities to create more new ideas and see them to fruition.

The main lesson I've shared with my children is that every opportunity in life leads to the next one and you have to make the most of your connections with people, use your skills and have a positive attitude. Getting to know people, learning from them and their strengths is one of the greatest skills you can teach your children. When you know and understand people and you are intentional about developing positive and reciprocal relationships or partnerships, you will do well in business and in life. It is a continuous learning journey and one that takes time to master.

Helping children develop positive habits and routines

One of the habits of an entrepreneur (and one I practice every day) is to develop routines and habits that help me stay focused and grounded. Journal writing is one habit I use to set intentions each day and self-reflect at the end of the day. But you don't have to be an entrepreneur to journal! Just as I suggested this for you as part of your self care routines, you can also suggest this to your children to get them started with helpful and healthy habits.

One of the ways you can start your journal is by writing down the seven areas of your life you want to master. These are the areas I focus on each day, with a short paragraph or intention for each:

1. Finance
2. Family and friends
3. Spirituality
4. Lifestyle
5. Career
6. Health/fitness
7. Relationship – with a partner, yourself or both

Set an intention for what you want to achieve or improve in each of these areas and how you will do this. It can be one or more words or a sentence that describes what you want to achieve. At the end of the day, check in to see how you went. When you do this every day, you will find that you become more conscious when making decisions or changes to improve in each of these areas of life. You will become more aware of your strengths and where you need to be more intentional and strategic to master each aspect of your life. This is one way to practice self mastery which provides you with more control over your life, focusing on holding yourself accountable for your decisions and how you want to navigate your life.

Your children may choose areas related to their learning, family, friends and interests. You can encourage your child to write down seven areas that mean the most to them:

1. Family
2. Friends
3. Sport
4. Reading
5. Organisation
6. Down time
7. Screen time

Ask them what they would like to focus on so it is relevant for them. When asking children to write an intention for each area they want to focus on, it might look like this:

> "Today I'm going to be a friend to someone I don't normally talk to"
>
> "Today I'm going to be focused in class"

Talking through intentions with your children is a great way to understand and get to know them at a deeper level, to be more aware of how they are thinking and feeling. If you only manage to do this once a week, that's great! It's not always possible to fit in things like this every day, but if you make it a habit, even if it's just one specific day during the week, it will make a difference for your child in learning how to create positive habits that impact their mindset and help them to understand themselves and their own behaviours. You may also like to set family intentions and individual ones that you share with each other.

In your role as guide and supporter of your children, it's important to spend time listening to your child's ideas and to be aware of their strengths. Every child is good at something and many different strengths. What they are excelling in can usually be what they enjoy the most. Perhaps a question you can ask your child or children is what their definition of success is and how you can encourage them to find their version of what that looks like for them.

There are many qualities that people need to become successful entrepreneurs – many of which we touched on earlier in the book as non-cognitive skills.

The most essential skills an entrepreneur needs include:

- **Courage** to be different and take risks, and to know how to manage when people disagree or challenge an idea.
- **Persistence** to keep going, even if you make mistakes, face challenges or meet people who don't believe in you.
- **Empathy** for others, especially when designing ideas that make a difference in people's lives.
- **Emotional intelligence** to understand other people and put yourself in their shoes, to understand challenges and develop solutions, to have self awareness and the capacity to listen or observe others' feelings and emotions.
- **Values and integrity** to develop ideas that don't just make money but help others along the way and help you stay true to your highest values and what you believe in.
- **Self awareness** to ensure you are able to manage yourself and your emotions and to access a balanced life.
- **Motivation** and self management to be disciplined.
- **Positive and optimistic** outlook regarding life and people.
- **Sense of humour** to not take things too seriously and remember to have fun while working and when having downtime.
- **Cognitive strengths** of strategic thinking, imagination, creative, critical and practical problem solving skills.
- **Resilience** to not take negative feedback personally, to learn from mistakes and see them as opportunities for improvement or to try something different.
- **A lifelong love for learning** to continually improve yourself and be willing to keep learning.

Supporting aspirations and career pathways

Do you remember what was expected of you as a child going to school and at home? For me, there were rules to follow and standards set to ensure I toed the line. At home, there were chores that my siblings and I were expected to do without question. We were given boundaries and knew when it was and wasn't ok to cross the line.

I often felt that I had to prove myself to my parents, teachers or other people who I thought had high expectations of me. I recognise now that it was only out of their love for me that they wanted me to do well at school and in life. If I failed, I felt that I was letting them down. In some ways this may have planted thoughts in my mind that perhaps I would never be quite good enough or meet the expectations of others.

Many people have spent their whole lives conforming to or trying to meet the expectations of others and in the process have actually let themselves down. Following the expectations of others can prevent you from moving towards and fulfilling your true purpose in life because it is easy to develop a fear of failure or even a fear of success.

As a parent, you want the best for your children. You want them to do well at school, to achieve good results, to gain a well-paying and secure job, and to be happy. Supporting them to reach their full potential and their goals means working with them rather than using a top-down or authoritative approach or projecting your expectations and aspirations onto them.

Not everyone is destined to be a doctor, rocket scientist or sculptor. Not everyone is suited to work with their hands or to teach others. Gradually, through a process of elimination in the schooling system, we realise what we are good at, what our strengths and passions are, and what really isn't for us. With so many choices available, it can be daunting to choose a career path, especially if students aren't fully aware of their strengths and interests. This is where your observations and guidance is critical to enable conversations with your children about their interests, aspirations and expectations, so together you can explore options for career paths that are suited to them.

Many young people are still unsure of what they enjoy or what opportunities there are beyond certain career choices when they reach the end of their formal schooling. I've had many conversations with sixteen and seventeen-year-olds who have no idea what they want to do when they leave school. Some feel pressured to choose a career they feel they should pursue rather than what they really want to do.

Choosing a career is a very personal decision, and one that should be talked about well before a decision is made at the end of school. You may start conversations in the early years of secondary school and listen to your child as they start to explore their options. They may change their minds several times before making a decision but at least having conversations about possible career choices shows them you are interested and that you are there to guide them in making a choice about and supporting them to achieve what they want to do.

There is nothing wrong with having expectations and encouraging the aspirations of your children. In fact, it is essential to have at least a level of expectation for them to achieve to the best of their ability, to push themselves just that little bit more to achieve their goals and to give themselves every opportunity or an edge in what is a competitive world. But ultimately it is their life and they need to gradually learn to take responsibility for their aspirations and expectations – with your support.

Helping children develop aspirations

To aspire to achieve means choosing to take steps to reach for those aspirations and aiming to achieve more than we might think we are capable of. For your children to have aspirations and dreams, and want to achieve them, they need your support and encouragement for the following:

Perseverance

This can start when children are young with small things, like not giving up when something is challenging. If they are losing a game or if they become frustrated when building or creating, you can encourage them to persevere, take a break and come back to it later to try again. Things don't always go to plan, problems aren't solved instantly. Things take time to accomplish and these are teachable moments that you can use to support your child to keep going and not give up.

Enjoying what they do

Take notice of what your children enjoy. What are their passions and strengths? You can encourage their interests by exploring things they can do that are related to their interests. If they love dinosaurs and facts, borrow books about these from the library or watch films with the topics they enjoy. If they love playing sports, support them by joining clubs and getting involved. If they love to build and make things, support this by making space for them to build and make. When it comes time to choose what they would like to do for a career, all your efforts in supporting their interests mean they may be more likely to know what they want to do and where their strengths are. When they enjoy what they do, and their values are being met, their working life becomes more enjoyable.

Encourage them to listen to their inner voice

When anyone decides to follow their dreams there will always be doubts – negative voices and other people's opinions that can convince you that what you are doing is wrong. Encourage your children to listen to their inner voice, the one that is positive rather than negative – if something feels right and they have thought it through and have a plan, there shouldn't be any reason for anyone else to interfere or for negative thoughts to prevent them from pursuing their goals. The stories you tell yourself matter the most when it comes to reaching for and achieving goals or choosing a different path. Ultimately helping children with decision making is a very important skill. Talking through how to make decisions, looking at the possibilities and the risks, the pros and cons and then working through how decisions will impact their life and others is a good way to help children understand they are making considered choices.

Encourage risk taking

Nothing is achieved without taking a risk. For many people, it is a risk to do anything outside of their comfort zone. Risk taking is inherent in most children – from the time they begin to walk when they are toddlers they tend to have no fear of failure. Taking risks, failing and getting up again to try again is one of the reasons many people are successful.

Fear of risk taking is one of the main obstacles to achieving what you set your sights on. When your child wants to try something new, instead of immediately focusing on the risks (within reason and as long as they are safe), encourage them to try it and see how they go. If it fails, it's a lesson not a disaster! In life there are so many risks that we have to take and if this is instilled in children when they are young, they are more prepared for what life has to offer and for challenges that may come along the way.

Encourage children to make a difference for others

As humans we thrive more as a community and when we have the support of others. When developing aspirations, one of those should be to make a difference to others, to the Earth or to the local community, as well as those within your circle of friends and your home.

Ask your child to think about how they can make a difference each day and include it with their daily or weekly intention. How can they make a difference either to another person, to the environment, at school or in the community?

This will inspire them to explore opportunities to make a difference as they grow. It is a simple way to show them how to aspire to improve their world and how they can contribute, even if it is in a small way. Imagine if every child thought this way every day and did something to help another person, or they did something to make the environment cleaner, calmer, brighter? The possibilities and impacts are endless!

Encourage self-belief and confidence

This is perhaps the greatest challenge when exploring your talents and skills. The little voice in your head that plants a seed of doubt can actually be quite crippling and can prevent people from moving forward in life to imagine and fulfill dreams.

This is an area that has interested me for a while, perhaps since I was a child – I struggled with confidence in my younger years and didn't really know what I was capable of until many years into adulthood. The idea of writing a book never crossed my mind until someone showed me that this was possible. I just needed to overcome self doubt.

Mindset and confidence are so important to nurture in ourselves as well as in our children to provide them with opportunities for their future. Our thoughts are the key to a positive mindset but we can only turn our thoughts around if we are aware of them and willing to take the action to change.

CONCLUSION

When you plant a seed of love, it is you that blossoms

MA JAYA SATI BHAGAVATI

I hope you've enjoyed learning about your very important role in your child's learning and development. Most importantly, I hope you have learned more about yourself and the need to focus on self love, self care and awareness so you are able to effectively support and guide those around you, especially your children.

Everything I've shared in this book has been to plant seeds of love, and to encourage you to do the same for your children. I have shared my own story and what I have learned while guiding my children. I hope that what I have shared will inspire you to nurture yourself and your children in their learning and growth so they are well equipped to be confident, happy, grounded and loving people for life. Many of these skills I learned as I grew to become a fully functioning adult – failing and overcoming obstacles, through research, teaching and working, through formal and higher education and some good advice and life lessons. My own parents taught me many things and supported me in various ways. Mostly what they taught me was to be independent and strong enough to weather storms and to discover what makes me happy.

No matter what your children choose to pursue in life, it is essential for them to learn who they are, to have self worth, self love, self belief, self awareness and self motivation to do what they feel in their heart is their calling. Teaching them to understand and know themselves is the best gift you can give your child. This brings them closer to their true selves, their intuitive self, so they are able to feel free to create and be the best version of themselves. To encourage them to be mindful and of service to others, including their future children. When they are given a sense of freedom to go forth on their own path and live a life full of learning and growth, knowing they are supported, they will be more capable of achieving what they want in life.

I encourage you to do the best you can, seek support, partner with teachers and your child, surround yourself and your children with positive influences, know you are not alone on this journey. We are all in this together and the more we can support each other, the more our children benefit. The journey through learning at home and school should be enjoyable and exciting for your child and for the whole family as it is a pivotal time in the lives of children. When you focus on the groundwork, developing the foundations, planting and growing the seeds, your guidance will have an enormous impact and you will know that everything you've done has been to fulfil your role in preparing your child to take the leap into adulthood.

I wish you well on your journey.

ABOUT THE AUTHOR

Rachel Stewart
Coach, consultant, speaker, author, parent engagement and cognitive learning practitioner

Rachel Stewart is passionate about learning, creating connections and new ways to solve challenges that make a difference in the lives of children. She specialises in guiding schools and parents through professional learning workshops, webinars, coaching and courses to embrace a culture of family and parent engagement in learning so that together, they can provide the support and encouragement children need to thrive in learning and in ife.

As a mother of three children, she has experienced the journey through school with her own children. She shares insights into how to navigate the many changes and growth of both yourself and your children to create connections, provide foundations and inspire them to thrive in learning and life.

REFERENCES

Abulof, Uriel. 2017. "Introduction: Why We Need Maslow in the Twenty-First Century." *Society* 54: 508–509. https://doi.org/10.1007/s12115-017-0198-6.

ARACY Parent Engagement Conference. 2017. Accessed 24th February 2022. https://www.aracy.org.au/blog/aspiring-to-inspire-reflections-from-the-parent-engagement-conference.

Armstrong, Kim. 2019. "Interoception: How We Understand Our Body's Inner Sensations." Association for Psychological Science. Accessed 10th March 2023. https://www.psychologicalscience.org/observer/interoception-how-we-understand-our-bodys-inner-sensations.

Australian Curriculum and Assessment Authority (ACARA). 2023. https://www.australiancurriculum.edu.au/f-10-curriculum/general-capabilities/personal-and-social-capability/.

Australian Institute for Teaching and School Leadership; Teaching Standards. Accessed 21 June 2023. https://www.aitsl.edu.au/standards.

Australian Student Wellbeing Framework. 2018. Accessed 10th February 2023. https://studentwellbeinghub.edu.au/educators/framework/.

Autism Speaks. "Sensory Issues." Accessed 21st March 2023. https://www.autismspeaks.org/sensory-issues.

Barker, B, and Harris, D. 2020. Parent and Family Engagement: An Implementation Guide for School Communities. Canberra: ARACY.

Barnes, M, Tour, Katrina and Babaeff, Robyn. 2019. "How school-family-community partnerships strengthen learning in culturally diverse schools." TeachSpace: A place for teachers to continue to learn. 2/12/19. Monash University Education. https://www.monash.edu/education/teachspace/articles/how-school-family-community-partnerships-strengthen-learning-in-culturally-diverse-schools

Benson, D. (1999). *A narrative inquiry of school and parent councils: A partnership and the promise of power or "hollow words"?* Unpublished doctoral dissertation, Simon Fraser University, Vancouver, BC.

Buckley, Flack, Clare, Schoeffel, Susannah, Walker, Lyndon, Bickerstaf, Amanda. 2022 Pivot Wellbeing for Learning Research – Evidence brief on student wellbeing from a pilot in schools.

Cain, Susan. 2013. *Quiet: The power of introverts in a world that can't stop talking.* Penguin Books.

Caspe, Margaret and Lopez, M Elena. 2014 "Family Engagement in Anywhere, Anytime Learning." *Harvard Family Research Project.* Accessed 15 February 2023. https://archive.globalfrp.org/publications-resources/browse-our-publications/family-engagement-in-anywhere-anytime-learning.

Catholic School Parents Australia. 2019 "Gearing Up For Parent Engagement in Learning Toolkit Launch." https://cg.catholic.edu.au/lat-news/gearing-up-for-parent-engagement-in-student-learning-toolkit/ & https://www.parentengagementcspa.edu.au/.

Cincotta, Katie. 2014. "Creative Smarts the Key to Career Success." *The Age.*

Permission has been given to reproduce elements of the article by Katie Cincotta.

Commonwealth of Australia or Education Services Australia Ltd. 2023. Student Wellbeing Hub. Accessed 14 March 2023. https://studentwellbeinghub.edu.au/educators/framework.

Conn, Rosemary. 2023. "A Wellbeing Crisis for Children." Accessed 14th March 2023. https://www.schoolsplus.org.au/campaigns/a-wellbeing-crisis.

Demartini, John. (2020) "The Breakthrough Experience: An Exceptional Opportunity of a Lifetime." Dr John Demartini and the Demartini Institute.

Demartini, John. "You Have Control Over These 3 Things." Accessed 15th March 2022 https://www.youtube.com/watch?v=AOrHsXrcCRI.

Department of Health, State Government of Victoria. 2021. Better Health Channel. Accessed 8 April 2022. https://www.betterhealth.vic.gov.au/health/healthyliving/wellbeing#about-wellbeing.

Dispenza, Joe. 2013. *Breaking the habit of being yourself – how to lose your mind and create a new one.* Hay House Inc.; Reprint edition.

Energia. 2023. Structure of Intellect SOI Certified Learning Manual. Singapore https://www.energiasoi.com/

Evans-Whipp, T, and Gasser, C. 2018. *Growing Up In Australia – The Longitudinal Study of Australian Children, Annual Statistical Report 2018.* Melbourne; Australian Institute of Family Studies.

Fleming, John and Ledogar, Robert J. 2008. "Resilience, an Evolving Concept: A Review of Literature Relevant to Aboriginal Research," *Pimatisiwin.* Accessed 11 November 2022. https://www.ncbi.nlm.nih.gov/pmc/articles/PMC2956753/.

Galinsky, Ellen. 2000. *Ask The Children, The Breakthrough study that reveals how to succeed at work and parenting.* Harper Paperbacks; Reprint edition. Harper Collins Global.

Gilmour, Mike. 2019. *The Power of Rapport, A practical guide to build trust, increase productivity and develop authentic connections.* Singapore: Partridge Publishing.

Goodall, Dr Janet. 2017. "Effective parental engagement is all about relationships." Connect Scottish Parent Council. https://connect.scot/teacher-professional/blog-space-educators/effective-parental-engagement-all-about-relationships-says-dr-janet-goodall.

Goodall, Janet. 2018. "Leading for parental engagement: working towards partnership." *School Leadership & Management*. 38:2, 143–146. https://www.tandfonline.com/doi/full/10.1080/13632434.2018.1459022.

Harris, A and Goodall, Janet. 2008. *Do Parents Know They Matter?: Raising achievement through parental engagement.* UK Network Continuum Education.

Harvey, Benjamin J. 2018. *Present like a Pro reference material.* Authentic Education Coaching.

Harvey, Benjamin J. 2023. "The Success Equation of a Billionaire Zen Buddhist Priest". Accessed 23rd July 2022. https://www.authentic.com.au/blog/wealth/the-success-equation-of-a-billionaire-zen-buddhist-priest.

Hattie, John. 2003. "Teachers Make a Difference, What is the research evidence?." Paper presented at the Building Teacher Quality: What does the research tell us ACER Research Conference, Melbourne, Australia. Retrieved from http://research.acer.edu.au/research_conference_2003/4/.

Hattie, John. 2008. *Visible Learning; A Synthesis of Over 800 Meta-Analyses Relating to Achievement.* Routledge; 1st edition.

Hattie, John and Anderman, Eric M. 2011. *International Guide to Student Achievement.* Routledge; 1st edition.

Hattie, John and Timperley, Helen. 2007. "The Power of Feedback." *Review of Educational Research.* March 2007, Vol 77, No.1 pp.81–112. http://rer.sagepub.com/content/77/1/81.

Haynes, Alison. 2004. *Change – How to kickstart the future and refresh the spirit.* Murdoch Books.

Heffernan, Amanda, Magyar, Bertalan, Bright, David and Longmuir, Fiona. 2021. *The Impact of COVID-19 on Perceptions of Australian Schooling.* Monash University, Monash Education.

Higgins D and Morley S. 2014. "Engaging Indigenous parents in their children's education." Resource sheet no. 32. Produced by the Closing the Gap Clearinghouse. Canberra: Australian Institute of Health and Welfare & Melbourne: Australian Institute of Family Studies.

Landsbergiene, Austeja. 2018. "Responsible parenting: Create memories, not expectations." TEDx Talk. Accessed 14 January 2023. https://www.youtube.com/watch?v=A71OktxTPac.

Levitas, Jennifer and Hurst, Melissa. 2021. "Jerome Bruner's Theory of Development: Discovery Learning & Representation." https://study.com/academy/lesson/jerome-bruners-theory-of-development-discovery-learning-representation.html.

Lodge, Michelle. 2022. "10 Successful Young Entrepreneurs." *Investopedia.* Accessed March 2022. http://www.investopedia.com/slide-show/young-entrepreneurs/#ixzz3nBOFfh7c.

Mapp, KL and Bergman, E. 2019. "Dual capacity-building framework for family-school partnerships (Version 2)." Accessed April 2022. http://www.dualcapacity.org.

Mapp, KL and Henderson, AT. 2022. "Everyone Wins! The Evidence for Family-School Partnerships & Implications for Practice." USA. Scholastic.

McCarthy, Bernice, St. Germain, Clif, Lippitt, Linda. 2002. "Reviews of Literature on Individual Differences and Hemispheric Specialization and their Influence on Learning" http://www.4mat.eu/theory-the-theory.aspx.

McGilp, J. & Michael, M. (1994). *The home-school connection: Guidelines for working with parents.* Portsmouth, NH: Heinemann.

Michalowicz, Mike. 2022. LinkedIn Post https://www.linkedin.com/posts/mikemichalowicz_repeat-after-me-the-job-of-an-entrepreneur-activity-6979875681132257280-1v6r/

Neuroscience Meets Psychology, Dr Jordan Peterson interview with Andrew Huberman, Accessed October 2022. https://www.youtube.com/watch?v=z-mJEZbHFLs&t=2681s.

Nguyen, Jordan. 2022. Keynote presentation: National Catholic Education Commission Conference, Melbourne. https://www.drjordannguyen.com/topics.

O'Connell, Megan and Watterston, Jim. 2022. "Those Who Disappear: The Australian education problem nobody wants to talk about." *The Age.* Accessed 27th September 2022. https://www.theage.com.au/national/victoria/lockdowns-are-over-but-anxiety-lingers-as-more-victorian-students-refuse-school-20220519-p5amrj.html.

Olszewska AM, Gaca M, Herman AM, Jednoróg K and Marchewka A. 2021. How Musical Training Shapes the Adult Brain: Predispositions and Neuroplasticity. *Frontiers in Neuroscience.* doi: 10.3389/fnins.2021.630829.

Online Etymology Dictionary. https://www.etymonline.com/word/rapport. Accessed 20 January 2023.

Parent Zone Scotland. Guidance on the Scottish Schools (Parental Involvement) Act 2006. Accessed 23rd December 2022. https://education.gov.scot/parentzone/getting-involved/scottish-schools-parental-involvement-act.

Payne, D., & W. Tirre. 1984. "Individual differences in learning rate." Paper presented at the Ninth Psychology in the Department of Defense Symposium, USAF Academy, Colorado Springs, Colorado.

Phillipson, Gervasoni and Sullivan. 2017. "Beyond Numeracy@Home: Supporting families during their child's transition to learning mathematics at primary school." https://www.numeracyathome.com/.

Pushor, Debbie. 2001. *A storied photo album of parents' positioning and the landscape of schools.* Unpublished doctoral dissertation, University of Alberta, Edmonton, AB.

Pushor, Debbie. 2013. *Portals of Promise; Transforming Beliefs and Practices through a Curriculum of Parents.* Canada: Brill Academic Publishers.

Pushor, Debbie, and the Parent Engagement Collaborative II. 2015. *Living as Mapmakers; Charting a Course with Children Guided by Parent Knowledge.* Sense Publishers.

Pushor, Debbie. 2020. Presentation for Catholic School Parents Victoria.

Pushor, Debbie. 2023. Walk Alongside Conference glossary. https://parent-engagement.ca/glossary/

Ricca Smith, Charlotte. "Bare Biology; Labelling parents; the good the bad and the downright unnecessary." Accessed 20th March 2023. https://www.barebiology.com/blogs/news/labelling-parents-the-good-the-bad-and-the-downright-unnecessary.

Richardson, Jodi and Grose, Michael. 2020. *Anxious Kids: How Children Can Turn Their Anxiety Into Resilience*. Penguin Life Australia.

Robbins, Anthony. 2023. "Discover the 6 Human needs; these core needs drive every decision you make." Accessed 21 March 2022. https://www.tonyrobbins.com/mind-meaning/do-you-need-to-feel-significant.

Robson, David. 2021. "Interoception: the hidden sense that shapes wellbeing." *The Guardian*. https://www.theguardian.com/science/2021/aug/15/the-hidden-sense-shaping-your-wellbeing-interoception.

Sari, J. 2018. "Goal Setting Theory of Motivation (Locke and Latham) explained." Accessed 15 February 2023. https://www.toolshero.com/personal-development/goal-setting-theory/.

Shakhovskoy, Marian. 2021. *Enhancing parent engagement in secondary school: An investigation of agency, dialogic learning, and intersubjectivity using Bronfenbrenner and Bakhtin frameworks*. The University of Queensland.

Sheffield Morris, Amanda. 2007. *The Role of the Family Context in the Development of Emotion Regulation*. Oklahoma State University. https://www.ncbi.nlm.nih.gov/pmc/articles/PMC2743505/.

Siegel, Daniel J and Payne Bryson, Tina. 2012. *The Whole-Brain Child: 12 Revolutionary Strategies to Nurture Your Child's Developing Mind*. Bantam; Illustrated edition.

US Department of Education. 2022. Announcement of National Parents and Families Engagement Council. https://blog.ed.gov/2022/12/u-s-department-of-education-announcement-on-national-parents-and-families-engagement-council/.

Vance, Ashlee. 2017. *Elon Musk: Tesla, SpaceX, and the quest for a fantastic future*. New York, NY: Ecco, an imprint of HarperCollins Publishers.

van Cuylenburg, Hugh. 2022 "About" The Resilience Project. Accessed 11 November 2022. https://theresilienceproject.com.au/about/.

Vorhauser-Smith, Sylvia. 2011. *The Neuroscience of Learning & Development White Paper; Crystalizing Potential*. Australia: PageUp People.

Waters, Dr Lea. 2000. *The Strength Switch, Standing for Strength in a World Obsessed with Weakness*. Australia: Penguin Random House.

Weiss, H, Lopez, M. Elena Lopez and Caspe, M. 2018. "Carnegie Challenge Paper: Joining Together to Create a Bold Vision for Next Generation Family Engagement." Global Family Research Project.

Winthrop, Rebecca, Barton, Adam, Ershadi, Mahsa, Ziegler, Lauren. 2021. "Collaborating to transform and improve education systems – A playbook for family-school engagement." Brookings. https://www.brookings.edu/essay/collaborating-to-transform-and-improve-education-systems-a-playbook-for-family-school-engagement.

World Economic Forum. 2022. "5 Skills kids will need in the future." Accessed 1 November 2022. https://www.weforum.org/videos/these-are-the-skills-kids-will-need-in-the-future.

Zhao, Yong. 2012. *World Class Learners: Educating Creative and Entrepreneurial Students*. Corwin; 1st edition.

www.ingramcontent.com/pod-product-compliance
Lightning Source LLC
Chambersburg PA
CBHW070353120526
44590CB00014B/1119